NINE HOUSES

CHRONICLES OF ONE WOMAN'S TRIUMPH OVER ABUSE, SHAME, AND NEGLECT

D1073032

MARY EATMON

AS TOLD TO JULIE EATMON

Editor: Ask Janis Editorial / Janis Hunt Johnson

Library of Congress Cataloging-in-Publication Data:
Mary Eatmon, 1931–
Nine Houses: chronicles of one woman's triumph over abuse, shame, and neglect / Mary Eatmon

ISBN: 978-0-9862667-0-6

Printed in the United States of America

Cover art & Interior Design by IndieDesignz.com

DEDICATION

To God, my heavenly father Jesus Christ. It is through His word that I learned: all things are possible.

To my parents, David James and Lillie Mae Plump: your integrity, love, and compassion instilled in my life have made me the woman I am. I never told you what really happened, which caused me to interrupt the life you provided for me, and for that I am truly sorry. My decisions catapulted me into a hard life of premature adulthood, with no warning and limited training. Unfortunately, I cannot take my life back. But if I could, I wouldn't, because my children mean the world to me and I am grateful for the joy they have given me. May you both rest in peace; I love you.

To my children Tanya, Gregory, Cary, Julie, Rhodesia, Michael, and Kim and my grandchildren. You are in my prayers. I may not have been the typical mother or grandmother, but that did not mean that my love for you all did not exist.

To my son Reginald (Ricky): may you rest in peace; I miss you so much and I love you.

George, You have been my son from day one. You've always been there when I had no one else to turn to.

DAUGHTER'S FOREWORD

Mary Eatmon: she's the most amazing woman I know. At age 83, she's just now catching up to her own wisdom. She has always possessed knowledge about things in life that have far surpassed her age. For years, I'd sit at the edge of my bed eavesdropping on some of the conversations that she would have over the phone with people who were distraught over the fact that the sky was falling in their world. But I knew that *she* knew that what they were going through would soon work itself out. She'd always say, "This too shall pass." For the longest time, I thought that she was quoting a line from a familiar poem; but she was speaking from her own experience. She walked her talk, walking those words out, in her own life.

When I got the call that she had opened her Pandora's box to release a 65-year-old secret—which she was afraid to do, even up to the day my father was placed in hospice care—I could have passed out. My brothers, sisters, and anyone with ears who heard her story that day were all stunned. Even now, when I close my eyes, I can still hear my sister Dinah as she broke the news, as if she were the newest anchor member on our local news: Momma had been raped at the age of 15 by DIDDEE! Immediately, it was as if everything that made me who I am had dropped like stones to the pit of my stomach. I was torn up.

As you read the memories of my mom, follow the twists and turns; travel the highs and lows; and laugh and cry with her. You will feel what she felt.

In the end, if you yourself are subject to abuse, when you understand that you no longer have to be a victim of your circumstances, you will be encouraged and empowered. You will want to make decisions that will turn your life around, like my mom did. I'm sure, if I weren't inspired to follow her example, I would not be the resilient woman that I am today.

—Julie Eatmon

ACKNOWLEDGEMENTS

As with any project, it takes a great team to make the plans of a book come together. I want to extend my personal and sincere thanks to those of you who encouraged me to write my story and to release the guilt and shame I've carried for the past 65 years. Thank you.

The contributions of many of my children's stories will now be read everywhere, and others will be delivered and set free from their plights, just as my children have been.

Many names have been changed to protect certain individuals' privacy.

TABLE OF CONTENTS

PROLOGUE

It was a day that began as though my life's story had been taken right from the pages of a children's bedtime story, complete with the sound of birds chirping and a beautiful radiant orange sun. Not a single cloud could be found in the blue sky, and you could smell the scent of flowers drifting in the air. I could not have imagined how such a pleasant and tranquil day could possibly end so horribly.

I once heard that when a person experiences an extremely traumatic event, as a result of emotional duress, the brain's defense mechanism is activated, allowing the individual to mentally separate consciousness from physical manifestation, thereby producing an out-of-body experience. The person is then able to completely disconnect from the trauma that is taking place as it unfolds, shielding the victim from the emotional, mental, and physical pain and suffering that are occurring in real time.

On this particular day, there was no such mercy to save me from the pain. I could only wish to have found such solace. Instead, I was forced to endure it all, knowing what was happening, but at the same time not understanding it.

Although the actual time that elapsed was only a few moments, it seemed as if time had literally ceased to exist, and I would be trapped in this nightmare for all eternity. After the deed was done, I could feel my former self melting away, like fog with the first rays of the morning sun. It was as if the girl in me had shed herself, and a heap of pain, soul, and innocence lay discarded on the floor beside me. All that was left was a shadow, a mere glimpse of the vibrant, wide-eyed, fun-loving 15-year-old I once was. As a result, a shadow would follow me—rearing its ugly head often as I grew into the woman I would become—seeping into every fiber of my being, long after the ordeal was over.

Looking back at that awful point in time, it's difficult to grasp that something as cherished and endearing to me as all my children could have resulted from such a long and heinous episode in my life. Now I can't say with certainty if my children and I were his first victims or not. I can only pray we were his last. Despite it all, it was easier than I had thought it would be to forgive, and to go on living my life. You never know what direction God intends for your life to take.

INTRODUCTION

Walter Dean Eatmon (whom we called Wadean), my ex-husband of nearly 30 years of marriage, had been discharged from Detroit's Veterans' Hospital with congestive heart failure. He would be living the remainder of his life in hospice care.

I remember it was around mid-September 2011, on a Thursday morning, when the Lord had awakened me and placed it on my heart to confront Wadean about his past offenses against me, and to forgive him for what he had done to our children. He needed to know how his actions impacted our lives. I suddenly thought very clearly: *I should tell him directly*.

Every week, our daughter Dinah would visit; but on this particular Thursday, when she arrived, I told her that I needed to tell her father something. So we decided to visit him the following Saturday. It was time to face this head-on and attempt to gain some sense of closure after so many years.

That Saturday evening when Dinah arrived, we drove over to see Wadean. He had moved into a house just around the corner from where we once lived. Where we parked, I could actually see an empty field where our house once stood on Virginia Park and 12th.

Just before we got out of the car, Dinah asked, "Ma, you sure you're ready for this?"

I turned and said, "As ready as I'll ever be." I couldn't help but stare blankly at the lot where our old home once stood, remembering all the pain the kids and I had suffered at the hands of Wadean.

As I was getting out of the car I drifted off into my own thoughts....

"MARY, DIDN'T I TELL YOU TO STOP TRYING TO GET ALL CHUMMY WITH THESE OL' NOSEY NEIGHBORS 'ROUND HERE?! THAT'S YOUR PROBLEM; YOU HARD-HEADED! I'M TIRED OF THIS MESS!"

Wadean had yelled loud enough to wake the dead. He'd then headed straight for our bedroom closet and started ripping all of my clothes from the hangers. He made a big pile in the middle of the floor as if they were all dirty. Tears welled up as I stood there in shock while pleading with him to stop this foolishness. But he ignored me as he knelt down and gathered up my clothes in a huge bundle and walked out of the room. By the time I realized what he was doing I tried to grab his arm to keep him from leaving the house; but in a fit of rage he clenched his teeth and said: "If you don't get your hands off me, woman—" Then he yanked his arm away from my grip and walked down the front porch steps holding all those beautiful new dresses that my mother had just bought me. Then he threw them out on the lawn as if they were trash. Embarrassed, I'd wanted to just crawl into a hole somewhere and not show my face ever again. I felt so ashamed and degraded. Even though his verbal attacks failed to draw a crowd from outside, many, including his own mother, peered through their windows.

I blinked away from my lapse down memory lane when I heard Dinah knock on the door.

Caleb, our youngest son, opened the door and replied, "Hey, Dinah," with a smile on his face. Caleb had taken on the responsibility of providing his father in-home support as his newly appointed care provider. The two exchanged a heartfelt embrace, and then his attention was immediately diverted to me as I stood behind her. "Mama, that you?" he asked with a look of surprise.

"Hi Caleb," I replied.

We made our way up to the second floor toward Wadean's bedroom.

"Diddee, you got a couple visitors," Caleb said as we entered Wadean's room. The smell of disinfectant and the stench of stale urine permeated the small room.

Caleb explained, "To give y'all a little update, he doesn't speak much nowadays, so don't expect a warm welcome. But he can hear just fine."

"Okay, that's fine. I just have something I want to read to him," I replied. "It won't take long at all; I'm sure he needs his rest."

I couldn't believe what lay before me. Wadean was a mere shell of the man he once was. Gone was the big broad-shouldered man I feared so much. His face had become withdrawn and gaunt; he had the body of a scrawny child, and he had aged even beyond his years from what I recall the last time I saw him. Seeing Wadean like this was quite a shock for me. It was all I could do to hold back my emotions and not shed a tear out of pure sympathy for this man lying in such a pathetic state.

I glanced at Caleb, as if to get permission to approach him.

Then Caleb said, "Go ahead, Momma. Like I said, he can hear you."

As he lay there, very quietly, I reached into my purse to pull out the letter that I had prepared; but, just before I began to read it to him I greeted him warmly by saying, "Hello, Wadean. I have a few words that I'd like to share with you. What I am about to say to you, there is no need for you to deny or admit to anything that I read; because I know everything I'm going to say to you is the truth."

Wadean,

The day you raped me I felt so violated and very ashamed. To this day, it still hurts my feelings that you desecrated my parents' bed and made me feel that it was all my fault. And the sad thing about all this is I didn't even know you, but because you said you would kill me and my entire family if I ever told anyone, I kept this secret for over 65 years. You robbed me from ever knowing what it would be like to fall in love for the first time and what true love is between a man and a woman. I never felt the warm embrace of a loving man who truly deserved me. Because of you I never remarried and had to live out my life as a single mother. However, my children were the only things you gave me that I could call my greatest accomplishment, even if you never appreciated that same feeling. Which brings me to another point of my dismay, our children. You never knew how much of a blessing those kids were.

Our children were amazingly gifted and they actually honored and respected you. They affectionately called you Diddee, and they all knew you were equally talented as well. But all you did for them in return was tear down their self esteem, belittle and humiliate them individually in unspeakable acts of immorality. You molested your own daughters and granddaughters, you shamed your sons unmercifully, and alienated the others, and you never looked back. To this day the scars we all hold are immeasurable and the love lost is just plain sad.

The irony of all your action is un-laughable because it was these same children who grew to become wonderful human beings who were also the ones who led us to accept our Lord Jesus Christ as our savior. Had it not been for their unselfish, loving and forgiving way, you would have been held accountable for all the evil you inflicted upon us. Wadean, you know these things I am saying to you is the truth and if you never acknowledged this day and what I am saying to you, just know I forgive you, and may God have mercy on your soul; and that is all I wanted to say. just know I forgive you, and may God have mercy on your soul; and that is all I wanted to say.

Mary

After I finished reading to him the one-page letter, I could see in his eyes that he had indeed heard every word I said. And although he didn't verbally acknowledge my letter—or even my presence for that matter—I knew he had fully understood. Dinah and Caleb stood there bewildered, not saying a word, but the expressions on both their faces spoke volumes. Up to this point, I had not shared my 65-year-old secret with anyone, not even my parents, as I had long ago resolved to take it with me to my grave. When my eyes met Wadean's, he glared back at me as if to say, *If closure is what you came for, then you came in vain.*

As Dinah and I stood up in silence, a new Mary had emerged: confident, triumphant, and most of all, forgiving. As we made our way to the front door, we hugged Caleb, and walked out of that house for good.

Reading my letter out loud was liberating; I was finally able to release all the pain, guilt, and utter misery that had plagued me for 65 years.

After we left, Caleb told me that his father did something strange. He said that Wadean took the white bed sheet that covered his body and pulled it up until it completely shrouded his face. He remained in that position for the next three days, refusing to eat or to allow anyone to visit. Staying true to his character, Wadean never apologized or owned up to anything that he had done to the kids or to me when we were married. Ironically, during that time, Caleb also mentioned that he overheard his father talking to himself. Out of the blue Wadean said, "I'm sorry that person did that to you." We now assume that he was imagining himself talking to me, and referring to himself in the third person, as if he still didn't see that he himself had been the attacker. After reading this book, I'm sure many people will say, *How in the world could this woman allow all these things to happen to her?* This is a legitimate question, and I will attempt to give an in-depth explanation of what actually happened to me and exactly how things turned out for me the way that they did.

NINE
HOUSES

CHRONICLES OF ONE WOMAN'S TRIUMPH
OVER ABUSE, SHAME, AND NEGLECT

CHAPTER 1

GOING HOME TO BOLIGEE

I really hadn't thought about that episode of my life for years, before I mustered up the courage to go through with confronting Wadean with my letter. I suppose what started it all was a small getaway trip down south that I had taken with my oldest daughter Tab and her husband, Bill.

Once I arrived at the Clearwater International Airport in Florida where Tab and Bill lived, we immediately set out for our road trip as planned, bound for Birmingham, Alabama. After a day's drive, we stopped in the town where I was born called Boligee, Alabama. Downtown Boligee was a far cry from what I had remembered. I hadn't been back there in years, and the changes I witnessed were a testament to my absence.

The bank and the adjoining pharmacy, which used to sit on the corner, were gone. Even the café, where I first saw a ceiling fan, was gone. I later learned that the people who still reside there do their shopping in the nearby towns of Demopolis and Eutaw. The only business left in this town was the old U.S. Post Office. Not much else remained, outside of the old railroad tracks that ran through the town.

I gave Bill directions to where my late grandmother Lillie's old house once stood. Once we arrived, I saw the place abandoned. Everything else around it had been bulldozed. I did see the old sawmill that still stood up on the side of the road; but weeds had surrounded its shabby structure.

When I think back to my grandmother's house, I remember my Aunt Martha. As a teenager, she would come home from school and teach my cousin Ann and me the latest dance craze all the kids her age were doing at the time. I could catch on fairly quickly to the steps she would show us, but cousin Ann just couldn't seem to pick them up.

Our next stop was further down the road, where my Uncle Johnny and Aunt Mary Plump had lived. They had an old creek that ran behind their house. I got out of the car and made my way over to the creek and knelt down. Everything was exactly as I had remembered it: the sound of the water running and the smell from the tall pine trees that lined the creek. As I looked closer into the water the only thing that I saw different was my own reflection staring back at me. The image in the water that peered back at me was not a young girl, but an 80-year-old woman. Looking in that creek brought back good memories from my childhood, leaving me with a sense of peace, happiness, and a longing to relive those early years; at least until I reached age 15, when my life changed forever.

Uncle Johnny's daughter Deatrice (we called her Dee for short) was my favorite cousin on my father's side. I spent lots of time at their house. This was the same house I had expected to be here now, but all that was left was that creek.

I remember one day, Dee fell in the creek, and I didn't know what to do. I was too young to have known how to swim. My reaction was to panic. I ran and told Uncle Johnny that Dee had fallen in the creek: I assumed she was drowning. They all rushed out to get her out of the water.

Thank God, she didn't drown, but she could have, because, like me, she couldn't swim, and I wouldn't have been able to save her. I laugh about it now because she was just bobbing up and down in the water as she yelled to the top of her lungs. Had she just stood up straight, she would have seen that the water only came up to her chest.

Unfortunately, Dee died early, at the age of 29 years old.

MOMMA MARIAH'S HOUSE

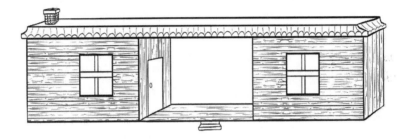

JUST OUTSIDE OF Boligee, Alabama, in Forkland, Alabama, was Momma Mariah's—my great-grandmother's—house. She lived in a unique two-room gray wooden house with a promenade connecting the kitchen, which was located on one end of the house, with the bedroom on the other end, each having its own door. There was an outhouse located in the backyard. I loved that old house so much; if I ever built my own, I would incorporate the layout of her house into a more modern one.

Momma Mariah was delightfully sweet, and an all-around beautiful person inside and out. In comparison to the rest of my father's family, who were mostly medium- to fair-skinned, Momma Mariah stood out flawless, with a complexion as black as coal.

She had a way of making you feel like you were the most important person in the world. You just couldn't help but love her. The charisma she had captivated many, including my grandfather, Papa Joe, widower to Mariah's daughter, Mary Delia, from whom I inherited my name.

Even though Papa Joe remarried a woman named Sarah, they, who lived up the road, both remained faithful to Momma Mariah, always providing food and supplies, since Momma Mariah had no garden and was unable to provide for herself.

The owner of the land that they all lived on was a nice white man named Ennis Thorn. He had a store in the cellar of his house. Sometimes Mr. Thorn would take us for a ride to check on his white-faced cows. They were so scary to us. He'd have us sit in the back of his truck as he made his rounds.

Once, when we were leaving Mr. Thorn's store, my younger brother Lee had gotten into a little mischief. He climbed into Mr. Thorn's truck and shifted the gear into reverse. The truck began to roll towards the pond. Lee jumped out of the truck and shot off running in one direction, and I ran towards Jim, one of the hired help on the land.

Thankfully, Jim reached the truck in enough time and the truck was not damaged. The funny thing is, the truck backed up into a tree, yet never had a scratch on it. No one ever mentioned what happened that day for fear of what might have happened to us.

CHAPTER 2

THE GREAT DEPRESSION

The Great Depression officially began on October 29, 1929, from that awful stock market crash. Its far-reaching effects, I can say, with a fair amount of certainty, passed by my parents, for the most part. Now, take into consideration the fact that my family was poor from the very beginning; and so was just about everyone else in our small town. So, what the rest of the nation was going through at that time was pretty much already the norm for us.

Life for me back then was what you could call pleasant and enjoyable. I was born on March 3, 1931. Then came my brother Lee, in May of 1932. Devon followed, in July of 1938. And last, our youngest brother Berry came years later to complete the brood in April of 1953.

My father, David J. Plump, was a very skillful man. In Boligee, he worked as a mechanic at a service station. Nowadays, they're referred to as gas stations, but back then, they really lived up to their name, because people never pumped their own gas—which on average, cost around 17 cents per gallon. My! Times sure have changed.

Both my parents were devout Christians who raised their children in the church, which is where my brothers and I spent the majority of our time. Daddy couldn't always make it to church with us because he worked on Sundays, but our mother took us to Sunday service faithfully, and sometimes even Bible study on Wednesdays.

As time went on, Daddy had gotten a little seniority, so he was able to start coming to church with us. Years later, he became a Deacon at our church. I remember when they celebrated his 50th anniversary on August 9, 1992. It was indeed a special event. There weren't a lot of people there, but it still managed to last well over four hours, most of which was filled with people just talking about the different things Daddy had accomplished during his tenure, and how faithful and caring he was to the church and its members. The plaque—which I still have to this day—reads:

Presented to Deacon David Plump, Sr.: Fifty years of dedicated service, at the Abyssinia Baptist Church in Ensley, Alabama; pastored by Rev. R. L. Patterson.

I still remember some of those in attendance joking around about how they planned to out-do Daddy, and celebrate being Deacon for even longer than he had. The recognition my father received makes me feel so proud as I look at the awards the church gave him.

My dad's characteristics—of being a man of integrity, kindness, and good looks, and of caramel complexion—made him stand out among many of the darker-toned men in town. Many women took note of him and questioned why he chose such a young girl to be his wife. But I believe that in his heart he knew that he had found his soul mate.

Back then, things were a lot different than they are now with regard to what age one ought to get married. With her mother's consent, my mother (Lillie Mae McAlpine) at age 12 married my dad (David James Plump), who was 19. He was a man of very few words, but he had a strong spirit and held strong to his convictions—to be a good provider and to hold true to whatever else he made his mind up to do—always completing his tasks.

It is my understanding that my dad did not have sex with her until she was well into her teens. By the time I was born, my mother was 15, and their relationship had blossomed. I am convinced that the type of foundation he laid allowed them to remain married for 74 years.

When I was about 12, we made the best out of our free time. While we didn't have a television set back then, we did have a radio. On Sunday evenings, we would all gather 'round the radio and listen to Christian stations. There weren't many, but we enjoyed them. I also enjoyed listening to the soap operas.

Daddy liked country music, which meant country music got a lot of play in the Plump household. My brothers and I managed to squeeze some ballads into the rotation, which is what we enjoyed listening to. I can recall how shocked our friends were when they discovered that we didn't know the latest blues songs, since everyone in our neighborhood listened to blues. One of our neighbors, Mr. Nelson, lived a few houses down, and he had a record player. He'd turn up the volume really loud,to where the whole neighborhood could hear Robert Johnson's *Crossroad*. No one complained about it, though. We just all knew he loved his blues songs. Some of my friends would even pretend to be inside a juke joint, and dance right out in the street to ol' Mr. Nelson's music.

Back when we lived in Boligee, on Saturday afternoons, my father would take our family into town. This is where all the people from the surrounding counties would come to mix and mingle. People were much more widely spread out than they are now. Some folks' closest neighbors would be 5 or 10 miles away.

I remember how much I looked forward to the weekends so we could go to town. There were a few small stores there with plenty of items to keep a kid happy. I would load up on enough candy and knickknacks to tide me over till our next trip into town.

There was a huge café that had a little of everything in it. You could get ice cream, candy, and even hamburgers and hot dogs. It even had a soda fountain with a soda jerk to serve us. They even had a ceiling fan to keep the place cool in the summer. That place was the first time I ever saw one, and I thought it was absolutely divine. I remember wanting one in our house, but I knew that was out of the question.

The kids would run around chasing each other and playing, while the adults talked about whatever grown-ups talked about back then.

Even though Madea (that's what we called my mother) did most of the cooking, Daddy could really cook, too. He was no slouch when it came to a home-cooked meal. If you found a man who could cook, then you had something really good on your hands; and my mom had found herself a keeper.

Just like Daddy, Madea really knew her way around a kitchen. She made sure we had something to eat every day.

Madea was a good homemaker. She had a hefty laugh that would brighten a room. A true lady in every sense of the word, she was both gracious and elegant, and she was known as a fashion-conscious woman. No one could wear a hat like she could.

She had a beautiful mocha complexion, and knew all the latest techniques in applying makeup. Madea also had a way of styling her hair that made other women often wonder who her hairdresser was. She'd smile, with her deep dimples, and tell them that she styled her own hair. Of course, women began to ask her if she'd be their hairdresser. Eventually, she began to build a small clientele of women who were in need of her unique services.

As Madea worked to build a stable clientele, she worked as a full-time housekeeper at the historic Tutwiler Hotel in downtown Birmingham. This was good money for her during that time, and it enabled her to help Daddy support our family.

By the mid-1950s, her confidence regarding her past education was low because she didn't read or write well; but because education was important to her and to her future as a hairdresser, she enrolled in a special program that allowed her to complete her high school education and earn a Bachelor's of Science degree in Cosmetology at the same time. This made Madea the first to receive a college degree in her immediate family. Once she received her degree, Madea happily opened for business in the new salon Daddy had built for her in the back of the house.

All this talk about my mom reminds me of the time when I was known throughout the neighborhood as "the little girl with a head full of hair." When I was about four years old, I remember getting ready to go to my Aunt Martha's wedding. Madea spent countless hours on my hair, which was very coarse, tangled, and long. As a result, she was only able to straighten half of my hair. Because we had no conditioner, she would sometimes heat a fork to straighten my hair for special occasions. For this occasion, however, since I was so tender-headed, she ended up balling up the rest of my hair in a bun. Had she not gone that route, we would have missed the wedding altogether.

CHAPTER 3

TOUGH TIMES

My father moved us up to a town called Ensley, a suburb of Birmingham, Alabama. On occasion, my parents would talk about how the 1929 stock market crash had affected our community. However, back when we still lived in Boligee, they said that they didn't feel the effects of the Depression, at least until after I was born. But in 1935, after we moved and settled in Ensley, they had begun to notice subtle differences.

Farms, gardens and livestock weren't as abundant. Because of the inner city's lack of jobs, the residents suffered more than those who lived in the country. Some had a hard time putting food on the table, and their overall mood was noticeably different.

People in Boligee, on the other hand, were pretty much self-sufficient. Many owned their own private land, they grew their own gardens, and they owned their own livestock. Chickens and cows were just as common as dogs and cats.

Before the stock market crash and the years to follow, Daddy worked as a carpenter. He didn't do it professionally, but he was skilled at it nonetheless, and picked up odd jobs here and there. Around the community, he had also become known as the watch repairman—repairing watches, as well as making casings for cuckoo clocks. This work helped to supplement his income during those lean years. Our parents managed to make it for a while, but because of the long-lasting effects of the Great Depression, jobs were not secure nor were they readily available.

When times really got tough, Daddy and Madea decided to send Lee and me back to Forkland, Alabama to spend time with Momma Mariah, until he could secure a more stable job. When we first got there, I must have cried for two weeks straight before I finally was able to accept the fact that my brother and I had to be separated from our parents.

Momma Mariah did the very best she could to help us. She instilled in us a strong church foundation, and we never missed a Sunday service at church. We stayed with her for almost a year. She made sure that she introduced us to her friends, and to their children, if they had any.

After my mother had my second brother, Devon, she came down to the country to see Lee and me. We were so happy to see her.

"Oh my, how you two have grown," my mother said as she hugged us both. "Pretty soon, you'll both be as tall as me," she said.

"We really miss you, Mama, and Daddy too. How long before we can come back home?" Lee asked.

Madea replied, "We miss you both, too—very, very much. It won't be too much longer now. Me and your father are already making plans to come here and get you both for good."

That afternoon was truly special because we had a chance to spend time with our mother after waiting for so long to see her. We hated to see her go, but we both knew that we would soon be one happy family again.

Since Papa Joe didn't live that far from Momma Mariah, we'd often walk over to his house and sometimes stay the night. Papa Joe was a sporty man, with a sense of humor that would brighten the darkest of moods. He liked hats and wore them tilted to one side. When he walked, it was with a smooth strut; he was definitely one cool cat.

He had a small farm with a cotton field and a huge garden with a few animals scattered about. I used to love feeding and caring for those animals. The heat, on the other hand, was often sweltering and I would try anything to keep cool, including walking barefoot. There was an old cow out in the field, named Bessie. On occasion, Papa Joe would send me to go out and "pull the cow," which meant I needed to bring her in from grazing where she spent most of the day. On his land there were sycamore trees with seeds the size of golf balls that fell to the ground. While walking, not paying much attention to where I was stepping, I made the costly mistake of stepping on one of those seeds. A sharp pain shot up my leg and traveled up to my arm in an instant. I yelled out so loud it scared the birds out of the trees. Needless to say, I never went to pull the cow again.

However, we still had to carry our own weight at Papa Joe's house. He always assigned us the chore of picking cotton. Once, when Lee and I stayed over, we planned to get up early the next morning and leave quickly, because we knew what was in store for us, and we wanted no part of it.

When we woke up, I went to Papa Joe and said, "Well, we're gonna go on home now, Granddaddy."

He replied, "No, you gotta eat breakfast first."

We both said in unison, "No, it's okay, we can just eat when we get home."

Then he said, "No, you gotta eat some breakfast, then pick some cotton before you leave."

We said, "We're not gonna pick any cotton."

But in a more stern voice, he said, "You're gonna eat *and* pick cotton, *period*! And you best not say another word!"

So after we ate, he gave us little pillowcases to fill with the cotton we picked; and though we didn't have much to pick, I believe he did it to teach us responsibility and to build our character, more than anything else; and then he took us home.

One of my fondest memories of staying with my grandparents was one time when Lee and I were headed to Momma Mariah's house from Papa Joe's. We ran into a snake. Lawd have mercy! Talk about walking on air. For years, Lee and I laughed about the incident until tears ran down our cheeks. But it wasn't because of the way we ran from the snake; it was because Momma Mariah said that the snake was dead the whole time.

Looking back on those times, I realize, life was so simple.

Finally, Daddy began working for the steel plant in Fairfield, Alabama. This particular steel mill was actually a subsidiary of the Pennsylvania Steel Mill, called Pittsburgh Steel. This is why they used to call Birmingham "the Pittsburgh of the South."

The time had finally come for us to be reunited with our parents. Uncle Johnny had the task of taking us back to Birmingham. He asked his friend named Sammie to come along for the ride. While en route to Birmingham, Sammie spotted a nice-sized rabbit alongside the road. Sammie just happened to have a .22-caliber rifle with him for hunting. He told my Uncle Johnny to pull over so he could try to shoot it. Uncle Johnny did as his friend asked, and five minutes later, we were back on the road with the rabbit in a bag inside the trunk of the car. Uncle Johnny then decided to make a slight detour and head over to his Aunt Laura's (who we called Big Ainnee), hoping she'd take the rabbit and make a meal out of it.

Big Ainnee lived between Forkland and Birmingham, so the stop wasn't out of the way. When we got to Big Ainnee's house, she greeted us all with open arms.

You know, it's amazing what people could throw together in a kitchen without the modern conveniences we take for granted today. Big Ainnee didn't have a gas stove, but once she got hold of the rabbit, she was able to whip up a rabbit stew that would make your mouth water. I still remember it to this day. It was enough to feed us four, along with her family as well; and we all had enough.

At last, when we made it up to Ensley, I hugged Madea and daddy for what seemed like hours. Plus, I had a brand new baby brother to smother with kisses.

It wasn't long after that, when Daddy enrolled me in Councill Elementary School, where I went straight to the 2nd grade. I was probably a bit old for the 2nd grade, but due to circumstances beyond my control, I missed a year of school when I had been sent down to the country.

HOUSE 1:
THE HOUSE ON 18TH STREET

WHEN I WAS ten years old, we already had moved to the house on 18th Street, when WWII broke out on December 7, 1941. It was a white duplex (back then, it was called a double-tenant house), with a large backyard, located on a busy city street. Once you stepped out onto our front porch, you'd see people walking, cars hustling, and hear the sound of the streetcar clanging.

Our parents made the best out of our home for my two brothers and me. At that time there were only three rooms: a living room, a bedroom, and a kitchen. My brother and I slept on separate cots in the kitchen, while our baby brother slept with our parents. The outhouse was in the backyard, just across the trench used for the city's water system.

After our next-door neighbors moved, our parents bought the entire duplex, and Daddy renovated it into a single-family home—with three bedrooms and one-and-a-half baths. The house was cozy. It was no time before our house became the talk of the town. After the renovations were completed, the living room and dining room alone were absolutely stunning. A few years later, Daddy added on a hair salon so that Madea could service her patrons.

Madea and Daddy were very loving, kind, and firm parents. When they spoke, it was the law. Their wisdom has continued to spread throughout our family to this day. Through Daddy's provision, he allowed us to have a place to call home. After 75 years, that house is still considered the family home, and my youngest brother currently resides there.

CHAPTER 4

MARY

The best years of my life were during the 2nd to the 8th grade, when I went to Councill Elementary School. Over time, I did so well in school that my teacher would ask me to read to the class as she crocheted during her breaks. By the time I started the 3rd grade, my mother needed me to watch my baby brother Devon. I loved school so much I'd pack a lunch for him and take him with me so that I would not have to miss a single day.

Once my teacher realized that I had to watch him, she told me to leave him with her while I went to my other classes.

A few short years later, I graduated as class president in January of 1946. Then I began my first semester at Parker High School. During those years, I never dreamt that I would not complete high school. Unfortunately, that dream of me graduating wound up taking 55 years to become a reality.

I was an adventurous child, so it didn't take much coaxing to get my brother Lee to come along on any of my numerous excursions. One day, Lee agreed to take a short trip with me. We had saved up enough money for bus fare to ride up to Birmingham to see what it was like. We had never been to downtown Birmingham alone. We were afraid to go too far from the bus stop; so, when we arrived we explored the main street. We looked into the large department store windows like a couple of snoops. We were so excited; we just laughed and giggled the whole time. We never told our mother or anyone about our secret trips.

I was now 15 years old, and still had much to learn about the world and life in general. I was just entering the 9th grade. I had a group of close girlfriends, and coincidentally, many of them were also named Mary. One of my closest girlfriends in junior high was Mary Menifee. We used to hang out together after school just about every day.

Once summer came, I would have gotten a summer job, like all the rest of the girls my age; however, Madea had a pretty good paying job as a maid, so we were pretty comfortable. She wanted to work instead of letting me work, so I could focus on my studies. She also wanted me to stay home and take care of my younger brothers. At the time, I was really disappointed. Not because I had to tend to my brothers, but because I couldn't go out and work like everyone else in my neighborhood. I was raised to do what my parents told me to do. I did manage to convince her to let me to work part-time on the weekends.

Racism in the south, at this time, had really begun to spread. Black folks still had to ride in the back of the bus. Everybody just accepted this as our way of life. There were a lot of white people we got along with really well; however, there were the other white people who made sure that we would never get our share of fair treatment. There were separate restrooms clearly labeled *Whites Only* and *Colored*; the same rules went for drinking fountains and restaurants. But my personal experience with racism never reached a level to where I was treated mean, or outwardly hated, because of the color of my skin. On the other hand, I still somehow knew things could have been much better.

There was a small bakery in our neighborhood that sold day-old doughnuts and all kinds of other pastries. We used to collect coupons and save them in order to buy certain items. Once, I saved up enough coupons to get a whole batch of day-old doughnuts. I asked Mary Menifee to go with me to the bakery. We were so happy, we made the mistake of taking the quickest route from the bakery through a white neighborhood, which bordered ours. That was the first and last time we ever did that. Those white kids threw rocks and shot their BB guns at us, until we finally made it out with no major damage to either of us. We actually laughed once we made it back home and devoured the rest of our treats; but it was pretty scary while we were being chased.

Around this time, Madea took a second job, working for a white woman by the name of Mrs. Rosa Cook. Mrs. Cook was very kind to all of us. I was able to wash dishes now, and I could do some light domestic duties. I would go over to Mrs. Cook's faithfully, every holiday. She'd cook a big dinner, and I would eat, and then clean the kitchen for her. She even allowed me to take a plate home if I wanted to, which I did quite often. We got along really well.

During the summer, my brother and I would go over, and he'd cut the grass while I cleaned the kitchen. We didn't have to go in through the back door or the basement, or use an outside bathroom, which was customary at the time. As a matter of fact, we could even go in and sit down where she and her family sat, and nobody would raise a fuss.

Her husband was a true Southerner, but he never mistreated us, or said any racist remarks to my family or to me. One time, Mr. Cook offered to take me home after a day of working in the kitchen for his wife. Well, I was prepared to hop in the back seat of his old Dodge, like I thought we were supposed to do; but he said with a smile on his face, "Mary, get on up here and sit down with me." So I sat in the front seat up with him.

You see, we had been programmed to believe that this was the way things were; and no one was trying to go against the system. Of course, later on, we did come to realize that it wasn't the way things should be, and people soon began protesting. We had learned how to live with the racism, and we all just dealt with it—until we could no longer take it.

A little after that, I was able to get some additional work as a domestic on Saturdays. I would help just about anyone who was in need of my services. I didn't limit myself exclusively to white people; I'd work for black folks just the same. There was a nice young black lady named Mrs. Jones, who lived down the street from us. She was pregnant at the time and needed help. I would sweep and mop her kitchen or whatever she needed done around the house. She only paid me a few dollars for the day, but I was glad to get it.

While working for Mrs. Jones, I had gotten the message that there was a white woman who needed help around the house, too. She wasn't too far from where I lived, so I decided to go to work for her also. Mrs. Lewis was her name, and she at least thought she was being nice to me. Mrs. Lewis had a daughter who was my age. Instead of having her daughter do the work, I guess she figured she'd just hire a black girl to do it for her. So as I worked, her daughter would not let me work in peace. The whole time, she'd follow behind me, bragging about how good she was in school and how smart she was. I'd just smile and nod my head and keep on working. At the end of the day, for doing everything Mrs. Lewis had told me to do, she had the nerve to give me two old rusty quarters. I couldn't believe it.

She was in no position financially to hire anybody. Well, I took my 50 cents and thanked her for it.

"You did such a good job, Mary, I'll see you around the same time next week," she said in a high-pitched voice.

I just smiled at her, and nodded. I said to myself, *in yo' dreams, you'll see me next week. I won't be coming back here ever again.* And I never did go back to that woman's house.

CHAPTER 5

WADEAN

One beautiful sunny morning, life as I knew it headed in a totally different direction, one that led me down a path that to this day continues to haunt me.

My parents were at work, and Lee had taken Devon down to the park to the local swimming pool. It was really hot in the house, so around noon, I went out and sat on the front porch. Someone nearby must have been cooking greens that day, because I remember the smell of collards drifting in the air, and it made me hungry.

You know, it amazes me that something can happen in one day—not over the passage of weeks or even months—just one single day can have the power to change someone's life forever. A big red Buick sped down the street, full of some kids that I recognized from the other side of town. I wondered where they could have gotten such a nice new car from, because I had never seen it before. Those whitewall tires from the car kicked up the dust from the street, as they were going so fast.

Just after they passed my house, I saw someone headed in my direction from the end of my block. At that moment, a huge bumblebee had me in its sight, but I managed to shoo it away with my hand. I squinted into the sunny, hazy day, and flashes of light glinted off the chrome bumpers of cars parked along the street, as I tried to bring the image into focus. Shielding the sun from my eyes with my hand, I was able to make out the figure now heading my way. It was a young man that I recognized from our neighborhood, named Walter, whom they called Wadean, walking on the opposite side of the street from my house.

As he got closer, he crossed the street, came over to where I was sitting on my porch, and began a friendly conversation with me. He was a tall and muscular young man, with dark skin and a well-manicured, government-issued crew cut. He told me he was only here for a short while because he was on his way to New Orleans for some Navy business he had to handle in order to get his discharge papers.

In a deep, monotone voice, he said, "It sho' is hot out here today. Could I trouble you for a glass of water?"

I replied, "Sure." Then I got up from the porch and headed straight for the kitchen.

I was 15 years old, and very naïve to the ways of the world, especially concerning men. I didn't realize that he had come in the house right behind me. Although I didn't know he was there, I could feel his steely-eyed gaze from behind. I assumed that he would just wait on the porch for me to come back with his water; but once I made my way to the kitchen, ran the water and turned around, he was right there, standing practically nose to nose with me.

I remember how shocked I was—that he was not only in the house, but that he was close enough to me that if he wanted to, he could have leaned slightly forward and kissed me. He didn't kiss me, though. He just stood there for a little while looking at me. I felt so strange, like a deer caught in headlights.

We were both silent for a while. Then I uttered the words, "Walter, what are you doing in here?" At that moment, a sense of dread washed over me.

He suddenly held me at arm's length and just looked me up and down, like I was a piece of meat. I knew right then that this man had dark plans for me.

Again I asked, "What are you doing in here?" It was all I was able to force from my mouth. But he didn't say a word. He just kept staring at me with a deranged look in his eyes. He grabbed me tight with his powerful hands and forced me into my parents' bedroom, which was adjacent to the kitchen. I tried to make a dash for the door, but he had anticipated my retreat and beat me to the spot.

With tremendous force, he shoved me against the wall to the right of the door. Then, with one of his enormous hands, he pinned my neck to the wall.

"Don't move," was all he said. With his free hand, he swooped underneath my dress and got hold of my panties, then yanked them off forcibly. He ripped them clean from my body, as if I were wearing a diaper.

Then he threw me on my parents' bed and I landed with a firm-sounding *whomp*. My head banged against the headboard and tears began to stream down the sides of my face, pooling on the insides of my ears. I tried to struggle only for a moment, until he wrapped both hands this time around my neck and squeezed till all the fight had left my body. Next, he lifted my skirt, and then I heard the sound of his zipper as he quickly tugged it down.

When I felt him penetrate me, there was a moment afterwards that I lost all feeling in my body. I struggled to say, "Get off of me," as I gasped breathlessly, while trying in vain to squirm my petite body out of this awkward position. But Walter would not stop what he was doing, nor pay any attention to me in the least.

I squealed, "I want my mama." I squawked, "*My Daddy will shoot you!*" Almost breathless, I then said, "*Please*! Stop this! This is *wrong*! Get out of our house!"

But my words fell on deaf ears, because Walter kept right on with his business as if I had consented to what he was doing to me.

I felt, for a moment, that I wasn't even there. Then it all came rushing back, only this time, the pain was much more intense, and I knew that all this was really happening. He was breathing so hard, he sounded like a big bull. I thought he was having some sort of an attack.

I remember the weight of his body on top of mine; I simply couldn't move while he was there. The pain that I felt while he was inside me was beyond words. I had never known of anything that could hurt that bad. An awful sensation shot through my whole body.

He had his way with me, right there on my parents' bed. To this day, this really hurts my feelings, that he desecrated my parents' bed. All I could do, at that time, was stare at the ceiling in my parents' room, and wish for the nightmare to end.

I can't remember all the details of what really happened, because I was so scared of what he'd do to me if I made any noise or tried to fight him back, so I just lay there.

I really was in a state of shock. It seemed as if I were temporarily paralyzed. I drowned in an ocean of thought, wondering, *how can I get out of this situation?* But there was no escape for me: *I've been raped.*

Once he had finished, he just got up off of me and stood there for a minute, and declared, "I'll kill you and your family if you ever tell anyone."

Next, he nonchalantly zipped up his pants and went into the bathroom to remove the condom that I didn't know he had on. Afterwards, he strolled out the front door just as easily as he had come in. He had obviously already plotted to do this act. He had been on the lookout for a victim, and I was an easy target.

It wasn't until years later that I realized Wadean was a pedophile. He had a fetish for young girls; and the older he got, the more intense it grew and the more he desired them.

After the door closed, all I could do was shut my eyes tight, as microscopic white specks of light flickered. I remember thinking they looked like little twinkling stars right before my eyes. The reason I couldn't recall screaming or resisting at all was because I realized that I *hadn't* screamed or resisted. All that yelling I did actually only took place inside my head. To my own surprise, I had temporarily lost the ability to speak. I just shut down.

The only words that I do remember saying to him out loud were, "Walter, what are you doing in here?"

I really had believed that I had tried to fight him off, and tried to scream; but the truth was, I was scared and as silent as a mute during the entire time that he raped me. The world around me, and all of its inhabitants changed into an enormous tomb, and for the longest time, there was nothing but silence, except for the constant pounding of my heart.

CHAPTER 6

RECOMPENSE

Before I knew what was happening, my mind worked like a movie running in reverse: Wadean grabbed me up from the bed and began walking backwards towards the spot on the porch where we had just been talking. Next, he made his way from the porch and crossed the street, headed in reverse back to the corner from where he had come. Then, the red Buick sped back by my house, only this time, in reverse, its tires seeming to inhale the dust from the street as if they were connected to a vacuum cleaner.

I imagine that he acted out his sick sadistic fantasies of luring a child. And little did I know that those fantasies would not stop with me. They would indeed continue to grow and fester, eager to claim the next victim.

I suppose, now that I look back on the attack, the fact that it keeps playing in reverse was my mind's feeble attempt to erase it from my memory, as if it had never taken place. My body and my mind seemed to be attempting to protect me, but only in vain.

Every time the hellacious episode reached the point where he got up off of the bed after having his way with me, the whole thing would just play in reverse once again. This same scene replays in my mind till this day. When I least expect it, it causes me to relive the attack. It doesn't haunt me quite as often now, but I do wonder if I will ever be able to press the stop button for good.

I cried endlessly as I fell back onto my parents' bed. After I managed to make it to the bathroom to refresh myself, I looked in the mirror and saw a victim staring back at me. My hair was a mess; my eyes were swollen and bloodshot from my tears; and my face was beet-red. I remember that my mouth hurt because I had never kissed a boy before. I was sure that making love wasn't supposed to hurt like this. I had never heard my mother say that she was scared and hurt after being with my dad. I saw it with my own eyes that he loved and protected her.

All I could think of, at this point, was to get myself cleaned up, as well as my parents' bed, which was now a bloody mess. Had they come home and found their bed in the shape that it was in, I was convinced that I would have gotten a whooping for sure.

To have gone through something as traumatic and mentally taxing as rape, I thought I had managed pretty well. Although I wasn't quite able to understand how something this horrible could have possibly happened to me, eventually I was able to wrap my mind around how I felt and what I needed to do next. Still in shock, I felt so violated. I also felt angry and ashamed.

I actually felt, at times, that it was my fault. I felt as if I had allowed this awful thing to happen to me. Of course, that wasn't the case; but the devil, which is an enemy of the mind, tried hard to convince me that it happened because of something I did.

All of my dreams, my plans, my visions, had been crushed in one fell swoop. Prior to that, I had ideas about what I wanted to be when I grew up. At one point, I thought that I wanted to be an actress, but the early black actors and actresses, in their limited roles, with wide buck eyes, had pretty much turned me off of that idea. I also wanted to be a singer. I had a beautiful voice, so I had been told. But that dream died after I was attacked.

I immediately began to think that this was the worst time of my life. In my mind, I had been soiled, robbed of my innocence by a man I did not know. On top of that, I had never even thought of being with a man in that way. I had no intentions whatsoever of doing that until my wedding night.

I automatically thought I was pregnant, and I didn't know how I would explain this to my parents. I was terrified to even utter one word about what had happened to me, so I didn't tell a soul. Besides the mental anguish I was forced to deal with, the physical pain that I endured was tremendous directly after the attack. But as the days went on, it got a little better. I couldn't believe that any person was capable of such a thing.

I somehow got in touch with Wadean through my neighbor across the street, Anna Hayes. It just so happened that Anna also knew Wadean through her boyfriend Al, who was a good friend of his. We were both talking about getting married: Anna to Al, and me to Wadean.

I was so naïve back then, I am ashamed to admit that I didn't know that it was extremely unlikely that I would have gotten pregnant during the rape, because Wadean had worn a condom. At that time, I had no idea what a condom was.

Had I known that I wasn't pregnant, I would have never even considered it—not for one moment—running off and marrying this man.

I never shared with Anna what Wadean had done to me; all she knew is that I wanted to get married. Somehow, Anna and Al had convinced Wadean to marry me. About a week later, we all ended up at the doorsteps of the Justice of the Peace for two ceremonies.

CHAPTER 7

NO WEDDING BELLS

On June 19, 1946, just two short weeks after the attack, we got married. From the very beginning, I was miserable. Every time I would think about it, I'd get physically sick to my stomach. It was nothing close to how I would have imagined getting married.

In a hazy, dreamlike state, I found myself looking at my signature at the bottom of that marriage certificate next to his, and, bewildered, I knew that it was indeed my own. We eloped in front of the Justice of the Peace, at the downtown courthouse in Birmingham.

After the ceremony, he told me he had to go handle some business, so he dropped me off and we went our separate ways. I crossed the threshold into my parents' house—not being carried by my new husband, but alone. This was my introduction to my new life as a married woman.

I entered the living room, and fortunately Madea was in the kitchen shuffling dishes and cooking as usual. I could smell the pleasant aroma of one her world-famous "sock-it-to-me" cakes, all throughout the house. The familiar atmosphere reminded me of how things were back when my life was normal.

At that moment, I thought: *This is not right. This can't be how a marriage is meant to be.* An indication of this startling reality was the fact that my parents didn't show this kind of distant love that my new husband and I supposedly had. *Love.* I don't dare even use the word. I didn't even *know* this man. He had taken something special from me that I could never get back.

I suddenly began to feel as if I had made the greatest mistake in my life. Because, at that moment, I realized that when a rapist attacks you, he doesn't love you, or even feel obligated to care for you. Now I agonized over this one thought: *If only I had just stayed in the house that day, when I first saw him coming up my block.*

A few years prior to the attack, I remembered going into our neighborhood corner store and seeing Wadean's pictures hanging on the wall. Come to find out, the owner's son, Sal, and Wadean were friends; after Wadean had joined the Navy, he'd sent Sal pictures of the places where he had been deployed.

During that time, I was a penpal to many of the soldiers who fought in the war. So when I saw his picture, I asked Sal for his address so I could write to him. But, for some reason, I had never gotten around to writing. I should have taken my reluctance to write him as a sign.

My brother Lee knew Wadean from the neighborhood, and on occasion I would see him in passing. At one of the rare neighborhood parties that I was allowed to attend, I greeted him through one of our associates. But simply because I regrettably engaged in a brief conversation with him on the porch, the following 30 years proved to be filled with grief and disappointment.

CHAPTER 8

WHAT DOES HE WANT?

From the very start, when Wadean threatened my entire family, he successfully instilled fear in me. He was a brutish man with a very large physique in comparison to my father. At the time, I thought that Wadean could easily inflict some serious damage on my father, who was of medium build, especially after witnessing first-hand what he was capable of doing to me.

I never once even heard Daddy raise his voice to anyone. He was a mild-mannered man, and I intended to keep the peace between him and Wadean. So I chose to keep my mouth shut.

Unfortunately, knowing God the way I do now, I can't really say what my father would have done; I realize now that I denied him his right to protect our family. For that, I am truly sorry. He died never knowing the pain that I have endured.

The next morning, after what should have been my honeymoon, Wadean came by our house and greeted my father.

"How you doing, sir?"

"I'm doing just fine. Don't I know you?" Daddy asked.

Wadean replied, "Yeah, uh, my name is Walter Eatmon, and I live up 18th street, and I've been away serving in the U.S. Navy. But, I'm home now, getting ready to be discharged." He was charming, adding that he'd served in the same platoon as our next-door neighbor, Mr. Haygood (someone I'd often written to).

Because Daddy didn't know what was going on, he returned Wadean's kindness with hospitality.

After a short while, Wadean explained that Mr. Haygood had asked him to deliver a special message to me personally to thank me for taking the time to write to him; and he asked if he could speak to me in private. Daddy begrudgingly agreed.

Madea, on the other hand, was more guarded and skeptical. She peered out of the front window, wondering what this grown man could possibly want with their daughter, and at that time of the morning.

Daddy called out for me, and I came from out back and walked towards the front door, and looked anxiously over at Madea.

Madea focused intently on the man who stood in front of her husband, like a mother hen guarding her chicks. Her eyes shot daggers at Wadean as he stood at the bottom of her porch. Her eyes narrowed to slits as she bit her lip, listening to every word he had to say. Once Wadean stated his request, Madea shot a cold stare at me as if she knew something wrong was about to happen, but she couldn't put her finger on it.

As Daddy entered the house, he insisted that Madea follow him to the back so that Wadean and I could talk. Only then did she relinquish her post as faithful guard dog.

As soon as they left, Wadean explained to me that he and Al had gotten a little too carried away with drinking that night. He stated that that they had been arrested and thrown in jail for public intoxication. For the first time, I actually looked at him as my husband, instead of as the monster who attacked me; and I thought: *With the type of burden that you have placed on me, how could you leave me on the day we got married, and run around the streets with your friend? You should have been here with me, to help tell my parents that we had gotten married!* Instead, I bit my lip to avoid saying anything, as I continued to think, *That's what you get for leaving me alone!*

Even though I didn't believe his story, I just allowed him to talk. But he insisted that they really had spent the night in jail, and that after they had both sobered up, they were released.

Next, he mentioned that he was leaving to go to New Orleans to get his formal military discharge papers, and that he'd be back for me soon. I agreed, because I basically wasn't quite ready to run off with him and be his wife just yet. At the time, I hadn't given any thought to the fact that he had raped me, or what a truly heartless man he really was. But I also thought that I was pregnant, and that I needed to take that time to prepare to be a wife and mother, and to figure out how I would tell my parents about our plans for me to move in with him when he returned.

I didn't know it at the time, but I found out later, that he also went to New Orleans because he had to go the hospital. He had contracted gonorrhea from somewhere, and had to be treated for it. Thank God, I was not infected then, nor was I ever infected during the entire duration of our marriage—a miracle, considering his philandering tendencies.

During the time that Wadean was in New Orleans, I stayed with my parents. After about two weeks, I was a nervous wreck. Madea seemed to be everywhere all at once. It was as if I couldn't escape her scrutiny. I could find no peace. I knew that I had to tell my parents about me being married—and soon.

I finally got to the point to where I couldn't bear it any longer. One night, when Daddy came home from work, I sat them both down and told them that I had married Wadean. I spared them all the gory details that had led to my decision; but I finally got at least that part off my chest.

Madea's rage was intense: "*Whaaaat?*! I'm having it *annulled!*" Madea exclaimed.

At that age, I didn't know that a marriage could be made null and void early on, let alone what the word *annulment* even meant.

"How could you do this to us, Mary?! Awe my Lawd Jesus! Why would you do this without talking about it first with us, baby?"

If only Madea had dug in a little deeper, and asked me point blank what made us decide to marry, then maybe I would have broken down and explained that he had attacked me. I wanted to say that he had vowed to kill them if I ever told anyone that he raped me. But her interrogation was absolutely brutal. Her constant onslaught of questions and condemnation seemed to never end. Each question came faster than I could answer. Finally, I held up my hands in surrender to end the onslaught. Her voice grew louder and louder at the reality of what her baby girl had actually done, without their knowledge or permission.

Sometimes parents need to allow their children to express themselves freely, without criticism. Back then, parents were the authoritarians and the children simply obeyed. In my case, had they actually allowed me to explain my logic, they would have realized that my story did not add up. For all I know, it's likely that they would have been prompted to confront Wadean about why we got married, and then they wouldn't have put all of their focus on their disappointment over losing me. I felt that they did not fight to keep me; but I was too scared to let them know that I was in real trouble.

The special bond between parents and their children should reach far beyond just the child's physical well-being. In the past, parents relied more on their natural intuition—their gut feelings—when their child was in danger or dealing with a real-life situation. Today, through constant awareness, our society has placed a stronger emphasis on understanding the traits of individuals who may be in trouble. Children now understand what to do when a stranger approaches, and parents are taught how to better communicate with their children, and what to do in order to protect their family from a possible attack.

As a rule, Daddy kept his composure, and didn't usually display a lot of emotion. But, on that day, things were different. I could see it in his face: the deep pain and anguish that I had caused him. I didn't have the heart to tell him that I had been raped. I couldn't bear to tell him that Wadean had threatened to kill him or anyone else if I dare told.

At that point, I knew that they wouldn't understand that I had made my decision to protect *them*; I wanted nothing more than to spare my family's life. At age 15 my rationale was to be their protector. I was frightened, but I felt that I had gotten myself into this dilemma, and I was the only one who could get myself out.

As Madea's rants continued like a downpour, I looked at my Daddy: tears began to force themselves from between his closed eyelids.

I had wished that everything could go back to how it was before, but it was too late. The reality was, nothing would ever be the same.

Daddy was hurt, and I hurt too, just knowing the grief that I had caused them both.

Madea finally sat down, swaying from side to side, as if she were tolerating shooting pains. Then she released a sound of anguish that pierced my very soul. As she sat at the kitchen table, she buried her face in her hands. She looked up at me with tears flowing like a raging river, as if I had stolen something she truly treasured: I had taken from her the opportunity to witness me growing up into the young woman that she was molding me into; she would never see me walk down the aisle, escorted regally by my father, on what should have been one of the best days of my life.

Madea began wringing her hands over and over, as if she were trying to remove a stubborn stain from them. When there were no more words left to say, after a while, she simply hung her head low and walked out of the room.

Daddy followed soon afterwards. But as he walked past, he placed his hands on my head as he swept a loose curl that had fallen in my face. He looked me square in the eye as if to say, *I'm disappointed, but I understand.* He followed Madea into the bedroom, collapsed on her lap and cried like a baby.

Just at that moment, my brother Lee came in and asked, "What's going on? Why is everyone crying?"

I told him that I had married Walter Eatmon.

With disbelief etched on his face, he asked for clarification. "You mean *Wadean* from the neighborhood? I know you don't mean that dude who just came home from the service, do you?" Staring me straight in the eye, he waited with anticipation, his mouth slightly open.

"Yes, that's the one," I replied.

Before I could say anything else, he yelled, "*You whore*! I hope he beats you! I hope he mistreats you in the worst way! I *hate* you, Mary!" Then he stormed out of the house, slamming the door behind him.

I never felt so alone in my life. Within a matter of minutes, I had torn my whole family apart. Everyone was crying. Everyone was so angry with me. I felt it with every breath I took. Everyone seemed to have abandoned me, which was crazy, because I was the victim in all this. But they didn't know that.

CHAPTER 9

LILLIE, YOU'VE JUST GOTTA GET PAST IT

The next day, with great anxiety, Madea and I talked about everything. Well, everything except for *how* I wound up in this predicament in the first place. I knew they were all hurt, but I wanted them to understand that what I had done was actually for the best. Time and time again, Madea persistently asked *why* I married him; but I was determined to keep my secret. All I could think of at that time was Wadean saying, "If you tell, I'm going to kill your family."

Now that time has passed, had I known what I know now—that he actually was a coward, I would have shouted from the roof top that I had been raped. It would have saved me from the many years of grief that were to come.

Our next-door neighbor, Mrs. Thomas, came over and my mom told her about my situation. I was actually glad that another adult, whom my mother respected, had arrived who would calm things down a bit.

"Well, Lillie Mae, you've just gotta get past it. After all, you and David got married at a young age," Mrs. Thomas reasoned.

"There's a heap of thangs that we did. But the difference between what Mary did and what me and David did is, I had *permission from my parents*. Mary *did not!*" Madea shot back.

When angry, Madea could be hard to convince in the beginning; but given time, she would most certainly agree with the voice of reason. And as predicted, after a while, Mrs. Thomas was able to bring her around to accepting it.

Back in those days, the entire sanctity of marriage was different, not just from the standpoint of the newlyweds, but from the parents' point of view as well. Back when Madea was around my age, people didn't really have the money to take care of a lot of children. Some families had children in droves, and struggled to take care of them all. In Madea's family, when a prospective suitor wanted to marry one of my aunts, my grandparents were pretty much obliged to give their blessing, to ease the burden off of their clan. The same was the case for my mom and dad; my grandparents willingly gave their consent, and all parties involved rejoiced and celebrated.

Even though of course this wasn't the case with Wadean and me, everyone eventually came around, and accepted the inevitable.

Keep in mind, during that era, people believed in keeping up appearances a lot more than they do nowadays. Many things took place behind closed doors (commonly known as "family matters"), to the point that outside the immediate family, no one else would dare meddle in others' lives, including the police. This was not an isolated issue for Blacks only; all people from every race dealt with similar issues and chose not to involve the authorities.

HOUSE 2:
THE HOUSE ON AVENUE T

MS. KATIE'S HOUSE—my mother-in-law's house—located on Avenue T, was gorgeous. It was painted white and had a huge front porch that provided ample shade on a hot summer's day. There was a large dahlia bush with beautiful blue-and-white flowers that bloomed from its well-tended leaves every summer. I used to snip a flower from that bush, and pin it to the side of my hair, just like Billy Holiday. On occasion, Ms. Katie would sit on a low stool to hand-pull each weed that had had the audacity to sprout up in her lawn.

She was a hard-working, frugal woman, who raised her own chickens in a coop behind her house. After her husband died, I'm sure that when she bought the house, she never anticipated the number of people who would call her house a home. The house seemed to literally stretch. There were five bedrooms and one bathroom. The problem was, there were at least 15 people in that one house at any given time, with never a moment's rest.

Ms. Katie was strikingly good-looking. The daughter of a German man and an Indian woman, her Indian lineage was apparent in her deep-set eyes and highly defined cheekbones. I was told, that as a young girl, both she and her baby sister were pulled from each other's arms, never to see one another again. I suppose that is why Ms. Katie seemed to bear many of the burdens of her family. Despite the fact that her late husband had been extremely cruel to her and their children, she was a woman with a big heart. That said, it still would have been a mistake to get on her bad side, because she had a quick temper, and her words could cut like a knife.

Living under these circumstances, with that many people, was quite new to me, since I had come from a fairly quiet household. I felt like I had moved into what seemed like a circus. For me, it was nothing short of hellish—hot, and full of mayhem. My poor nerves were rattled at first, but after a while I managed to settle down.

Besides her young sons—who, by the way, had no strong male influence whatsoever—there were no other men or any family members whom Ms. Katie could rely upon. It would take another book to describe the different activities that went on at her house.

Suffice it to say, the time we spent with Ms. Katie was not how I thought married life should begin.

With so many families under one roof, we somehow managed to function without stepping on each other's toes. We worked it out using unspoken schedules, one of which was with regards to cooking, where one day I had managed to get an opportunity to bake my first peach cobbler. It was delicious. But when I mentioned to one of the neighbors up the street that I had baked a pie, she asked to see it. Boy, that was a big mistake, because we both managed to devour the entire pie.

I told Wadean that I had baked the cobbler; but when he asked where it was, I had to tell him that we had already eaten it up. He shot back, "What the hell you tell me for then, Mary? Shoot, woman! You got my mouth all watering for a slice, and you done ate it up!"

I remember once back in 1947, delivery boys came to our neighborhood and passed out free samples of a newly innovated clothes detergent called Tide. Boy, there was a lot of trial and error using that product. Everyone had the darndest time trying it out, including me. The first time I opened the box, I poured the entire contents of the package in the washer. I had stepped out for what seemed only a few moments, and when I returned, bubbles had overrun the washer. It was a scene right out of that 1963 Doris Day and James Garner movie, *The Thrill of it All!* Soapsuds were everywhere! Talk about a mess! I thought I'd never live that down. I got teased for some time after that. But eventually, I got the hang of it.

CHAPTER 10

MARRIED? YOU'RE ONLY FIFTEEN

By the end of that summer, when school was about to start, I was ready to go home to my parents; but I knew there was no chance of that happening. I was, after all, married now, and I had been taught that a woman's place was with her husband. If I hadn't feared the repercussions of returning home to my parents, I would have considered an attempt at making my plea. At the time, I saw one unsolvable problem: Wadean. I did not want to jeopardize my family's lives if he found out that I told them that he had raped me.

Another remarkable fact that I later found out about was that Wadean was already engaged to a woman who lived up in Cincinnati, Ohio. Weeks after we had been married, I found out that his alleged fiancée had discovered that he wasn't coming back for her. She had written him a letter, which he casually mentioned to me.

He said, "Mary, she cussed me out real bad, and called me everything under the sun."

I didn't comment about it, as it was just another of his offenses, which I chose to ignore in order to keep the peace. To be frank, I was just too young to handle issues like this.

While living with Wadean, I learned to bury a lot of secrets. Things that occurred, we just never even brought it up—as if it had never happened. In all the years that we were married, he never apologized about what he had done to me in my parents' bed.

Still, early on, I did muster up enough courage to set some boundaries, stating with conviction, "Look Wadean, you can never use me as a punching bag and be beatin' up on me anytime you feel like it. And you cannot stop me from going to visit my parents. And another thing, don't ever try to stop me from going to church." Wadean agreed, and that was that. Little did I know that my nightmare was nowhere near over.

During my first few months of living in total upheaval in Ms. Katie's house, I had developed severe headaches. They had gotten so bad, Wadean had to rush me to the hospital. After many tests, the doctor explained that I was suffering from migraine headaches. Funny, I thought the headaches were a direct result of me being pregnant. But since the doctor never mentioned that that was the case, it confirmed my earlier gut feelings—that maybe I wasn't pregnant after all, because I had not missed a period in the two months I had been with Wadean. The doctor prescribed some medicine for me, and explained that I might or I might not have another episode. I'm not sure if the migraines were a result of all that was going on around me, or if the headaches would have come even if I had been at home with my parents. I just knew that I needed it to be quiet, and that the room needed to be dark, for me to feel better. But neither darkness, nor quiet, were ever made available to me the entire time I was with Wadean and his family. I eventually recovered from the headaches, and thank God, so far, I haven't had another episode since then; but that one time was definitely enough for me.

Over time, after I recovered, I settled into my new life as Wadean's wife. I also gave into my wifely duties and let him do his business on me. I grew used to it. Believe me, he and I never built a strong enough bond to ever fall in love with each other. Yet, I was determined to stick it out, because I had caused my parents so much pain and grief. (And even if I had gone home, at that point, I would have had to confess that I was raped, and once again live in fear of Wadean carrying out his promise to kill my parents and my brothers.) On top of that, I truly felt that since he had soiled me, by taking my innocence without my permission, then he should be forced to take care of me.

Have you ever met someone and imagined how life would be with that person? Well, for me, it happened when I went back to school that fall after I had moved in with Wadean's family. I met a young man at Parker High, someone I had never seen before. He sure was one handsome fella. He was one of the first boys I would have very much liked to introduce to my parents. His name was Harold. When we met, it was he who saw me first. He went out of his way to make sure our paths crossed that day. I actually thought that I could make our friendship work; but no, that was not to be. I quickly realized that no other man could ever come into my life now that Wadean had me as his wife. He had no problem with making his presence known to any man within sniffing distance. And I hated that.

When I told Harold that I was married, he didn't believe it.

"How in the world could you be married? You're only fifteen," Harold said in disbelief.

It took me forever to convince him, especially since I didn't have a wedding ring at that time, to prove it. After a few days of Harold's admirable attempts at pursuing me, or what we referred to back then as "courting," he finally gave up. He saw that I was sticking to my story of being married.

I often wonder how different my life would have been had I ended up with Harold as opposed to Wadean. Unfortunately, that's something I will never know.

Towards the middle of the semester, I realized that I wouldn't be able to remain in school because I had just about taken up permanent residence in my mother-in-law's bathroom just after I found out that I was pregnant with our first child. (None of my other pregnancies that followed turned out to be as bad as that first one.) I decided it would be best if I just dropped out of school all together. Remember, during that time, as far as I knew, there was no female birth control, or any education given to prevent teen pregnancy.

I managed to carry my first child full-term. But, unfortunately on May 12, 1947, our first daughter was stillborn. I named her Diane. The doctor said that she had a knot in her umbilical cord and there was nothing they could have done to prevent it.

Walter said that she was a pretty little brown baby, with a head full of dark, curly hair. I felt sad and depressed for a long time after that.

Everyone noticed my mood around the house during that time. One day, Ms. Katie came to me and said, "Mary, you may be crying for this one; but believe you me, you'll be crying a lot more if you keep having babies." She couldn't have made a truer statement.

CHAPTER 11

WADEAN, LET'S MOVE

Wadean's mother didn't live very far from my parents, but I didn't dare invite them over for a visit. I didn't want my parents to see how I was living, nor did I want any type of confrontation between Wadean and my father. Had my parents ever come over and witnessed all that drama, I'm sure there would have been a problem.

From very early on, I knew that Wadean wouldn't have the normal, loving-son-in-law type of relationship with my parents. My father never did like Wadean, even after getting to know him. And Wadean never cared for my parents. He never even tried to be a good son-in-law to them. He'd talk to them briefly, but that was it. There was never any legitimate love or affection between them. I had come to accept that this was how things would be among those three.

Not long after I had moved into Ms. Katie's house, the city had built some new houses about a mile or so from where his mother lived. One day, I asked him, "Why don't we get one of those new houses?"

He replied without giving it much thought. "Oh no! I don't wanna move! We gon' stay right here till we save up enough money."

Wadean and I both knew full well that we would never save any money as long as we lived practically free at his mother's house. Wadean had been working at the local steel plant in Ensley. The pay was great, and it would have been enough for us to afford one of those new homes, but I quickly realized that he was unmotivated.

Over time, I would soon find out that Ms. Katie played an integral role in Wadean's decision-making process. And the role that she played didn't necessarily have my best interest at heart. Wadean's refusal to move us out on our own the entire time was due to her influence. I tried my all to get him to move, but he wouldn't budge.

The closest we came to having our own place while we were there was when we rented a room for three months from a woman named Mrs. Jones.

"I'm going back to my mama's house. I ain't stayin' here another day," he exclaimed after that third month.

So we packed up the few belongings we had and moved right back in to his mother's house, where things had only begun to go from bad to worse for me.

CHAPTER 12

YOU'RE NOT MOTIVATED

Soon I was pregnant again. I gave birth to our son, Miguel, in December of 1948. Miguel was a bundle of joy. I had worried constantly throughout the entire pregnancy, fearing that this one would end up the same way that my first had, but God saw fit to bless us with a beautiful healthy baby boy. It felt so good to give birth to a healthy baby. All of my fears of another unsuccessful pregnancy were washed away as soon as the nurse put my son in my arms.

Wadean, on the other hand, could find no happiness. A dark cloud seemed to hover above his head at all times. Although he was a new father, he showed no drive, motivation, or vision. Nothing seemed to get Wadean going.

And the sad thing is, he was actually talented.

It was at this time that Wadean's friend, named Bay-Walter, had returned from Chicago to try and persuade Wadean to join him in the entertainment industry, as a comedian. Wadean refused to even consider it. As funny as he was—this path would have been a cinch for Wadean—he wouldn't venture out to try anything new. Sad to say, this wasn't Wadean's last time that he would end up turning down a wonderful opportunity.

Years later, when we moved to Detroit, a friend of his, named Jackie Wilson, told Wadean that he should give singing and show business a try, because if he could do it, then so could Wadean. As talented and popular as Jackie Wilson had become, to be honest, Wadean could outsing Jackie any day! Yet, he let the gift of singing go, without even *attempting* to pursue it. He never wanted anyone to see the gifts that he truly had. This was a heavy burden on me. I really tried desperately to encourage him. I just couldn't find a way to motivate him in the least.

Because of the different temperaments of all the adults in Ms. Katie's house, I felt like a hostage among strangers. We, along with the rest of his family, lived packed as tight as sardines. There were so many people under one roof, I just wanted to run and hide, leaving everything and everybody behind. But there I was.

Wadean and his brothers did actually have a bright side. They were all really comical when they wanted to be. They certainly liked to keep the family entertained every chance they got. Wadean had a way of saying something so funny, you'd burst your sides in laughter. So even though the laughter didn't outweigh my misery, there were some good times on Avenue T.

For a little over a year, we'd often go over to my cousin Pearlanne's house, where we'd join one other couple and dance the night away. The wife of the third couple was nice, and didn't mind us visiting. But, later I found out that she and her husband were having marital problems. Adding fuel to the fire, I later found out that she and Wadean had begun an affair.

About a year later marked a new phase in my life. I started working. It wasn't necessarily because I needed it financially, but I just wanted to get a break from being cooped up in the house. Downtown, there was an all-white cafeteria. It was there that I learned to balance two trays at one time. I was one of several black waitresses who waited near the cashier to carry the diners' trays to their table. This was an eye-opener for me because I began to see, on a regular basis, the disgrace of racism in action.

Meanwhile, outside of us socializing with my cousin Pearlanne, I often felt trapped and hopeless. So much so, on occasion, I'd leave and go spend time in Pittsburgh. One time, when Miguel was six months old, I took him and stayed with my Aunt Martha for three whole months. While there, I found a job working at a black-owned restaurant named M&M Soul Food. It was a good job to have, and the people were nice, and the food was good. I was always hungry, I spent most of my earnings on the food; I was now already pregnant again.

I felt as if I could live in Pittsburgh and start my life over again; but I had to deal with the fact that my marriage was unstable. I was a young woman with a small child, and another one on the way. I would often wonder, who would want to care for me with two extra mouths to feed?

The following May, 1950, after I returned to Birmingham, I gave birth to my second son, and named him Joseph (we called him Joe). He was such a happy baby. Neither Joe nor Miguel ever gave me any problems.

CHAPTER 13

LOVE LOST

Looking back on everything now, I see that Wadean not only stole my innocence, he robbed me of the better part of my entire childhood. While the rest of my friends were involved in attending all the school dances and house parties, and eventually, the prom, I was stuck with Wadean, cooped up in his mother's house.

For better or for worse, my fate had been tied to Wadean's. All those childhood things that the rest of my friends got to experience, I only got to imagine. Despite sacrifices I made when I moved in with his family—becoming a new mother, and dealing with the alienation I felt from living in that house—he didn't seem to love me, or even *like* me, for that matter.

Obviously there were opportunities for me to free myself from Wadean. For instance, when he raped me, I should have told my parents that very same day, instead of cleaning up the evidence. But, at the time, all I could think of was the threat he made. Then, when I found out that I wasn't pregnant, I should have packed my bag and never looked back; yet, I didn't want to address the aggravation that I had caused my parents, considering Madea's initial reaction.

I see now that surely they would have taken me back in, and gotten the marriage annulled; but my teenage shame got in the way. In those days, when a person got into trouble, it was expected that if you made your bed, you'd have to lie in it.

Was this a marriage built on fear? Yes, it certainly was. But once I realized that I would never have a chance at true love, I decided to make the best of a sad situation. I, like many, also misinterpreted the scripture in Matthew 19:9 that states, "And I say unto you, Whosoever shall put away his wife, except it be for fornication, and shall marry another, committeth adultery: and whoso marrieth her which is put away doth commit adultery." The truth was, Wadean had been untrue to our marriage for years. And if I did remarry, I would not have been the guilty party.

I was indeed free to remarry; but I was too young to know any better. For so long, I believed that by remarrying I would have been an adulterer, so I missed the opportunity to accept love into my life. Today, people get divorces and remarry as often as they buy new shoes.

Now that I know the truth, I would tell a person to just be sure you are marrying the right person the first time around. This way, you will avoid all the surprises in a marriage later on. It's important to pay attention to all of the red flags before deciding to say "I do."

CHAPTER 14

RACISM

Weeks unfolded into months, which eased into years. Before I knew it, I had been living with the Eatmons for nearly five years. It was during this time that I began to work on the weekends for a white couple named Ken and Doris.

They were the nicest people you would ever want to meet. We three were the same age, so we had a lot in common. We got along so well that Doris would happily prepare lunch for us and I'd eat at the table with them. This went on all the time; but unfortunately I got another dose of just how things were in the South. One day Doris' mother decided to stop by, and she happened to see us all eating together. You should have seen the look on her mother's face; we were just as stunned as she was. You would have thought someone had just committed a murder instead of just eating a quick meal. Needless to say, that incident put an end to our open lunch settings.

Up to that point, aside from the kids throwing rocks at me when I was younger, I had no problems whatsoever as far as racism was concerned; but after that visit from Doris' mother, there seemed to be a racial divide in that house where none had existed before. The following weekend, Doris and her husband began to eat their lunch separately from me. I knew that her mother was responsible for Doris' new outlook on race relations, but I shrugged it off as a sign of the times, and continued to do my job. Doris did pay well, after all, so I decided to grin and bear it.

That was just about as close to home that racism had gotten for me. Now, of course I knew about all the horrific things that were going on all around me in other states, and even in my own hometown; but I was never directly affected by the hate that was rampant during that time, until then. I was really proud during the Civil Rights Movement of the 1960s, when brave people, both black and white, began to stand up for what was right and demand equal treatment.

Even though I wasn't personally involved in the protests, I was still proud of everyone who did participate. When Rosa Parks stood up for us, by sitting down, that was a huge blessing. It showed how people could come together for a just cause and bring about positive change.

CHAPTER 15

I'M NOT YOUR PUNCHING BAG

Wadean lost his job at the steel plant, and that put him in a sour mood. He would mope around the house all day, with a dour expression on his face. From time to time, I'd try and cheer him up, but there was no way I could break through the wall he had surrounded himself with, just a few weeks after he had gotten fired.

My friend Evelyn and I were walking to the local theatre to see a western. While at my parents' house, Wadean called and told me to come home because he had something to tell me. I told Evelyn to go on without me, and I would catch up with her after I found out what he wanted.

Evelyn looked at me strange and said, "You sure, Mary?"

I said, "Yes, yes. Go on ahead; I'll catch up." But I had a feeling in the pit of my stomach that I wouldn't catch up. I could sense something was wrong by the tone in his voice.

Once I got to Mrs. Katie's house, I knew there was trouble brewing. Pure rage was in his eyes. As soon as I stepped through the door, Wadean yelled loud enough to wake the dead, claiming that I had been too friendly with the neighbors.

"Mary, didn't I tell you to stop trying to get all chummy with these nosey neighbors 'round here?! That's your problem; you hard-headed! I'm tired of this mess!" He then headed straight for our bedroom closet and started ripping all of my clothes from the hangers. He made a big pile in the middle of the floor as if they were all dirty, and then he walked, while holding all those beautiful new dresses that my mother had just bought me, and threw them all out on the lawn as if they were trash. Just after I gathered my clothes, I followed him back into the house and he started in beating on me, right there in his mother's living room.

Earlier, Ms. Katie had walked across the street to a neighbor's house, and peered through their window.

One of his brothers, Will, whom we called Moochie, wound up coming to my rescue. Moochie had a difficult time pulling Wadean up off of me. Wadean was Moochie's younger brother, but he was much larger than he was. By this time, Wadean had me pinned to the hardwood floor, sitting on top of me, while he slapped and punched me in my arms and face. He had thrown me all over that living room before he got me down and continued to pound on me.

Chairs were broken and tables were overturned before Moochie was finally able to get him off of me, and he even had to defend himself, because Wadean had reared up against him as well. Wadean was such a brute. The whole time he was beating on me I asked, *What did I do to deserve this?*

I'm sure Moochie eventually told their mother about the incident, and I know she must've seen something from across the street; but I never said anything to her about it, and she never mentioned it to me. I don't know what would have happened, had Moochie not been there to get him off of me. I could barely stand up straight; but Moochie helped me to the room that I shared with Wadean, and he gently placed me on the bed. I don't remember having any bruises, or a black eye or anything like that, but I distinctly remember how dizzy I was after it was all over.

Meanwhile, Wadean just stood there, looming over me like a monster. Through the whole ordeal, I later found out that Ms. Katie had planted a seed of discord in her son's head, telling him that I had my eye on one of the neighborhood boys. I truly believe she had left the house that day just so her son could beat me, because as luck would have it, other than Moochie, there was no one else in the house.

Several months after the incident, I decided to take a break and go back to Pittsburgh and stay with my brother Lee. Ironically, at the time I did not leave him because of the abuse, but because he wasn't attempting to do anything to improve our lifestyle.

To be honest, I was too afraid of him and what he might do to our kids and me. I kept telling myself, *I need to tell him that I am not coming back.* But I constantly kept putting it off, thinking, *I'll do it tomorrow.*

Eventually I started seeing a young man named Paul. I actually liked him; he and Wadean were as different as night and day. Paul treated me royally and showered me with compliments and affection, often telling me how proud he was to be seen out in public with me. Wadean had focused only on tearing me down, hardly ever taking me anywhere in public. In fact, on the few occasions that he did decide to take me out around his friends, he'd spend the entire time degrading me and putting me down in front of them.

I know that fear had a strong hold on me. I was petrified of what Wadean might do. Yet I struggled constantly to break it off with him, because I didn't want to have any more of these problems in my life.

I know now that I should have just told him, and dealt with the consequences right then.

Paul would often tell me, "Mary, you need to just be upfront, and tell this dude you're not coming back."

It had gotten to the point to where Paul would ask, "Did you write the letter today, Mary? You need to write that letter."

I went so far as to tell him, "Okay, I'll do it. I promise I will," but I never got around to it, because I thought I would wind up falling flat on my face and then be forced to come crawling back to him.

I should have just told him, "Wadean, I'm not happy, and I'm not coming back."

Knowing him, he probably would have said, "So what! Don't let the door knob hit you, where the good Lord split you!" I think what really made him come looking for me was his sense of pride. Certainly we both knew that he did not love me.

Somehow, Wadean must have gotten word that I was in Pittsburgh. One day, he just showed up. When Wadean arrived and found out that I was seeing someone else, he was mad enough to spit fire. The end result was dangerous. He and Paul wound up having words. Those words led to a knockdown, drag-out fight that got out of hand. All I could do was sit there helplessly and watch.

Eventually, someone called the police, and because Wadean had gotten the better of Paul, he was the one who was carted off to jail.

Despite the fact that he lost the fight, Paul didn't press charges. But, for one brief moment, when Paul looked at me, it became apparent to both of us that I was never going to be able to leave Wadean, no matter how badly he treated me.

I thought at the time that I had no choice. Based upon my Christian values, I mistakenly thought that divorce was a sin, especially if there were any evidence of infidelity. So I returned to Alabama with Wadean, unaware that the grounds for a divorce had already been set in stone—by him, not me. And, of course, the truth is, God would never have punished me for leaving.

In the article *Police Family Violence*[1], it mentions that in those days, if a woman called the police on her husband, she was not taken seriously, and was even considered radical. It was thought that women were challenging male entitlement to rule in the privacy of their own homes. It wasn't until the Women's Movement of the late 1970s that

---

[1] Wetendorf, Diane. "Police Family Violence: An Historical Perspective." Las Vegas, Nevada: Presented at the National Center for Women & Policing, Annual Conference, 1998. http://www.abuseofpower.info/Article_NCWP.htm

the issue of domestic violence entered the public arena. By definition, domestic violence is a so-called "family matter," which occurs in the seclusion of the home. When domestic violence laws were passed across the country in the 1980s, domestic violence became a crime.

There are still many women who say, "I can't call the police on him. I can't have my own husband arrested. I can't betray my lover, my husband, my friend. He isn't a bad person, it's just that he's under a lot of stress." A woman may say, "he has a bad temper," or "he only hits me when he's drunk." Or, she may say it's actually *her fault*—that she provoked him. A woman may feel that she must protect him, because he trusts her not to tell, not to get him into trouble; and, she still loves him.

The police and the states' attorneys find these remarks naïve and frustrating. They have little tolerance for these excuses for criminal behavior. They want these men held accountable in a court of law. The state, the police, and the domestic violence advocates tell these woman that a partner has no right to beat her—no matter how much stress he's under, no matter how much he drinks, and no matter how much he professes to love her and trust her.

It used to be that police officers were often reluctant to enforce the law against domestic violence, because breaking up "lovers' quarrels" and "marital disagreements" was not police work, and that police should not get involved in "family matters." Over time, most police officers today have come to consider domestic violence well within the range of legitimate police work.

The most profound way we can interrupt the cycle of violence is to hold the violent man accountable—to reveal the "family secret." A man who commits domestic violence will not seek help unless he is forced to, by someone else—by a woman who loves him, and loves herself enough, to leave the situation.

If you find yourself in such a situation, I encourage you to reach out for help, and to call the police if your partner hurts you. The police will protect a victim of violence, and the state will supply legal avenues for relief. Domestic violence advocates will provide emotional support. I urge you to come forward with the truth, so that you'll get the message to the abuser—and to the community—loud and clear: domestic violence will not be tolerated.

CHAPTER 16

MOVING TO THE MOTOR CITY

Times were really beginning to change. Wadean lost yet another job, as a maintenance man. He finally decided to take the advice of a few of his friends who had left the South for greener pastures up North, in Detroit.

As soon as we had gotten settled back in Alabama, Wadean took the boys and me to my mother's house, and then he packed up and moved to Detroit. The big three automobile companies (Ford, GM, and Chrysler) were in the midst of a huge hiring explosion, which had caused an exodus for many folks out of Alabama and several other Southern states, all looking for work.

Wadean had gotten a job at a parts distribution center, working as a technician. Since it was never even discussed when he would eventually send for me, my mother finally scraped up the money for me and the boys to catch a one-way train on up to Detroit.

Madea said to me, "Now Mary, you need to go on up North with Wadean. He's your husband after all, and a woman's place is with her husband."

So I contacted Wadean and told him I would be joining him soon. A few days later, Joe, Miguel, and I made the long trip north on the last day of 1951. Wadean met me there at the train station, and we began our life together as a family in Detroit, Michigan.

HOUSE 3:
THE HOUSE ON
CLAIRMOUNT STREET

WE WERE ABLE to find a room for rent at a boarding house over on Clairmount Street, from a nice woman named Mrs. Taylor. The homes in Detroit were much bigger than those in Birmingham. During this time, the Whites were leaving Detroit as if it were infected with the bubonic plague, so this meant that many houses were up for grabs.

It was a great big ol' brick two-family flat with a balcony. She rented out each of the three bedrooms. The living room, dining room, and kitchen were more spacious than those of the houses back home.

The grass was well-manicured; however, there were no flowers out front to brighten up the place. Yet it didn't matter, because we were still fortunate to live in such a place.

I was particularly fond of the windows that surrounded our spacious bedroom. When Wadean was gone, I would just sit and soak up the sun in the mornings as I dreamed of how I wanted my life to be. I'm convinced that the room was originally designed to be a library. The only thing missing were the books that would have lined the walls.

On summer nights, it was nice to sit on the balcony under the stars and look up and down the busy streets. As far as I was concerned, this was complete serenity. At least until the other two families that we shared the flat with came home. But even then, that was nothing compared to the ruckus we had been in with his family back down South.

Mrs. Taylor didn't live in the house herself, but her son and his wife, along with their two small children, lived in the lower flat. Mrs. Taylor's daughter-in-law had a way of speaking that was absolutely melodic. In fact, to hear her speak, you would have thought she was singing, her voice was so pleasant. You should have heard her croon with such bravado, for her daughter, Patti: She would pronounce it "*Paa-teee!*"

Surprisingly, the other two tenants in our flat turned out to be wonderful neighbors. Agnes and her husband, and Mattie (who proved to be a great help to me) and her husband, lived down the hall. Then there was Geneva and her son, who lived in the basement apartment. Geneva and I hit it off from the very beginning, and remained friends for over 30 years, until she moved back to California.

CHAPTER 17

TRANSITIONS

Detroit was a far cry from what I was used to in Alabama. When the boys and I first stepped foot off that train, we were met with conditions that we were nowhere near ready for. January in Detroit was like living inside a freezer: it was *so* cold.

Detroit was booming during the 1950s. There weren't many cities in the nation that were as wealthy or had grown as fast. Just knowing I was in The Motor City made it even more alluring. There were close to two million people in the city back then, and the Big Three was a major draw to hard-working folks from all across the nation. And I was glad that Wadean happened to be among the fortunate ones to land a job with one of the Big Three during that time.

Detroit represented a new start. I felt much freer once we got there. I suppose that feeling came from my liberation out from under Ms. Katie's roof. Whatever the case, I felt the hope of a new beginning, and it was refreshing.

The whole atmosphere here was new and exciting, compared to the South. There wasn't the same sense of fear that came over you when you were in the presence of white people. Even though you still felt isolated as a person of color, nevertheless it seemed like there was much less tension in the air. Besides the fact that I no longer had to sit in the back of the bus, I still had to acclimate myself as to what exactly constituted racism in this new place.

I had never seen so many people as I had in Detroit. Even the few times I had gone to Birmingham, there was no comparison to the amount of people and traffic that dwelt in this city. The people in Detroit, furthermore, seemed to go at a much faster pace than in the South. They didn't take time out to relax and socialize with one another, so it seemed.

Back home, you didn't feel so rushed to get here and there. Even at Ms. Katie's house, there was still some sense of camaraderie amongst the neighbors. Another difference I noticed between the North and the South was with regard to the black people here. They were much colder and distant towards me, not very friendly at all. I never did put a finger on exactly why that was, but I learned to deal with it. During my first few months, I assumed that I would not make any friends here. It was as if no one wanted anything to do with me for some strange reason.

Regardless of the challenge of building friendships, I was ready for a new life. I was 20 years old with two small children, and now another one was on the way. Because of the things that I had gone through, I felt much older than I was. I managed to make the best out of our new life here. With only a few months to go before my baby arrived, I spent a lot of time entertaining myself reading novels.

CHAPTER 18

I'LL NEVER CALL YOUR HOME AGAIN

During the time Wadean stayed in Detroit, he moved in with his oldest brother Mark (we called him Brah). Once he picked us up from the train station, Wadean took the kids and me to stay with him there. Considering where we'd come from, living with Brah wasn't all that bad. In fact, it was a great improvement from our time living with Wadean's mother, to say the least. Still, the best thing about living with Brah was that it didn't last long: we were there for about only two weeks.

What I didn't know at the time though, was that while me and the boys were down South waiting on Wadean to send for us, he was in Detroit, living the life of a single man. He had met a woman and told her that he was in the process of a divorce (which couldn't have been further from the truth). I found out about this little fling because the woman, named Sara, actually called one day, and I happened to answer the phone.

She and I talked for a while. Nothing nasty or unpleasant was spoken from either of us. She explained that she didn't know that Wadean not only still had a wife, but two small boys as well.

Throughout the entire conversation, we remained civil.

"Mrs. Eatmon," she said, "He told me that you were separated and getting a divorce. This is the only reason why I called. I thought he lived alone with his brother, and I had no clue he had a family down South." After I had told her that we weren't divorced, nor had we ever discussed separating, she said, "Well, I am so sorry, and I promise you, I'll never call your home again."

And she never did.

CHAPTER 19

POLICE ESCORT

Our sons were growing so fast before our eyes that I was amazed. Miguel was becoming a very smart little boy. I actually believed that Mrs. Taylor's daughter-in-law had got a hold of him and had taught him how to speak just as eloquently as she did. Miguel spoke so well in fact, Brah would come over and pay him just to talk.

By the age of four, Joe had become very active. He was your typical boy: full of curiosity and mischief. Once, while I was in the kitchen, I heard a loud commotion outside. I rushed out to the balcony and saw a group of city workers huddled in the yard. Right in the middle of them was Joe. I called out, "Joe, what are you doing outside, boy?" I rushed downstairs, with my eyes as wide as the moon.

"Ma'am, your son just fell off the second-story balcony," one of the men said, as he handed me my son.

When I heard this, my heart sank. I thanked the man, then immediately rushed off to the emergency room to make sure that he hadn't broken any bones.

Thank God, he hadn't, but he sure was shaken up. Come to find out, Joe had landed in the dirt part of the driveway. Back then, the driveways were not completely filled in with concrete—only the areas where the tires would set. To this day, I can still see it, even though Joe has since gone home to be with the Lord.

Wadean continued to grow more callous as our family grew. This caused me tremendous pain, because it was really sinking in, my realization that I would never experience true love. The first time I had ever had feelings for anyone was when I was only eight years old. Back in my old neighborhood, there was a boy named Belva, who was a few years older than I was. He and I made a real connection. I have never felt this way about anyone except for him. I can still recall every detail of his face. The last time I saw him, we moved the following week. I was hurt to my core, because I really wanted to get to know him, and I knew I would never have that opportunity. To add insult to injury, I later found out that he had drowned in a whirlpool in a creek, only two weeks after we moved. I truly believe that he was the one for me. My heart still aches for him.

During this time, I began to notice that Wadean was staying out more often. A few times, he even stayed out overnight. I never confronted him about this, or asked where he had been. I just didn't want any problems. I didn't want to give him any reason to reenact our last violent confrontation. Whenever he decided to come back home, he would pretend that he'd never stayed out overnight. He just went along as if everything was as it should be.

In April of 1952, when the time came for David to be born, Wadean, of course, was nowhere to be found. I didn't know what to do, so I asked Mattie for help. She said, "Call the police, and they'll take you to the hospital."

Herman Kiefer Hospital, located on the corner of Byron and Clairmount, was a state hospital for the poor—and it showed. The conditions at the hospital were deplorable, but that's where all of the black folks went in those days. The patients looked miserable. Their sad countenance told stories of their own.

As I was being wheeled in, I overheard the nurses talking about how I had been dropped off by the Detroit Police. Even though I had gotten fairly used to it, I was still embarrassed and hurt that I couldn't find Wadean. He never did show up for our third child's birth. Those hateful nurses had no idea of all the things I had gone through or the predicament that I had found myself in at that time. I was just trying to make the best out of a less-than-ideal situation.

I was so tired from this particular labor that it affected the time it took to actually give birth to my baby. I was in hard labor for close to ten hours. After a while, a heavyset white nurse burst into my room. She came in to check on me, but I could hardly focus on her because of all the pain I was in. I do remember hearing her squeaky shoes as she entered my room.

She didn't ask me my name or tell me hers. She just cut into me, like I owed her money or something. "Look here!" she said, "You should have had that baby by now. If you don't hurry up and pop it out, we're going to have to just clear this room out for someone else. *Do you hear me*?! You're not that special. We can't just put everything on hold until you feel like birthing your child!"

She spoke to me with such disdain that for a moment, I wondered if she was really an employee of the hospital or if she had just come in off the street to harass me. I got so upset from the way that she was yelling at me, I started crying. One of the doctors in the room even asked, "What's her problem?"

Right before I had a chance to give her a piece of my mind, she turned on her heels and strutted right out of the room just as fast as she had entered. I got so mad at her, within minutes of her verbal attack, I delivered my baby out of pure rage. And from this difficult delivery, I was extremely sore, and the lacerations from the delivery lasted for several weeks.

After a while, once I had a chance to calm down, I realized that the mean nurse was actually sent in there as a strategy to induce my labor. Her negative attitude had provoked me enough to give birth.

The accommodations were not adequate for even the most destitute. Back then we didn't have the medication or methods that are used today. Women were forced to experience the pain and agony. There were no showers, so new mothers were forced to share bathroom sinks in order to clean themselves. It was up to us to make ourselves as comfortable as possible.

The young woman whose bed was next to mine was around my age. She shared with me her story, which was quite similar to my own. She told me that her husband hadn't bothered to show up. She had given birth to their daughter, whom she had named Delilah, to spite her husband. We laughed about it to each other, but on the inside, I knew, she was hurting just as much as I was. That feeling of abandonment is something that no one should have to go through.

For a moment, we just looked at each other. We each recognized the emptiness that stared back at us. We both hurt because we were being neglected. It was wrong to be here alone, with no support from our husbands. As our tears welled up, simultaneously we nodded an affirmation that we would both somehow get through this.

Before coming to the hospital, I had made arrangements for Miguel and Joe to stay with Mattie. I thank God for her. There were no cell phones back then, so I couldn't call Mattie to let her know what was going on. I wondered what she thought of us as parents, leaving two small children with a stranger for seven long days. To top that off, I later learned that Joe contracted chicken pox, which was a total nightmare. Although Mattie was kind enough to watch the kids while I had the new baby, I know she didn't intend on looking after a sick kid, and taking a chance that she might get sick herself.

On the seventh day, it was time for the baby and me to go home. Wadean miraculously emerged from his self-imposed exile and managed to come to the hospital just in time to pick us up. When I got home, Mattie told me that Wadean had not been home to get the boys—not once—the entire time I was away. At that point, I guess I had become numb to all his foolishness. I didn't ask him where he had been, nor did he offer to fill me in. We just left it alone.

Even though I had David, the newest member of our family, nestled in my arms, I knew that nothing had changed as far as Wadean was concerned. He was indifferent. It was as if he'd just picked me up from the grocery store or something. He showed no emotions at all. Wadean was young and careless, and totally lacked the proper mindset of a husband and father of three. His only concern at that time seemed to be hitting the streets and doing God knows what. I believe that Wadean's mantra was, "I keep my wife barefoot and pregnant." It seems I had been reduced to exactly that.

In the following month after I gave birth to David, Memorial Day came. Wadean had been out earlier in the day, and I spent the time with my boys as usual. To my surprise, he came in with a slab of ribs that he had bought. He wanted me to make the side dishes to go along with it while he grilled the meat. You should have seen me getting to work.

After the food was cooked, he drove us to one of Detroit's best parks, Belle Isle, which was uniquely situated between Canada and the United States, at the Detroit River. That was my first time ever going to a park that beautiful. And, it was one time that Wadean truly surprised me. That day I was so happy. Years later, I learned that the architect, Frederick Law Olmsted, who designed Central Park in New York, also designed Belle Isle.

Not long after David had turned six months old, I felt strong enough to work. I found a job at a small Jewish restaurant on 12th Street, not too far from where we lived. Later on, I began working at another small café called Hazel's Chicken Shack. Just as I was beginning to get into the groove of working, I had to let that job go. Wadean had gotten me pregnant once again. This time we had our first girl. I named her Tabitha, and we called her Tab for short.

HOUSE 4:
THE JEFFRIES PROJECTS

WADEAN DECIDED WE needed to try out a place he had heard about at work, called the Jeffries Housing Projects. I had never heard the term "the Projects" before, so I was clueless as to what to expect. It actually wasn't all that bad back then. The drugs and crime, which the buildings later became notorious for, had not yet consumed it.

The Jeffries (East) Housing Project, located within approximately a 2½-mile radius from Tiger Stadium, the Masonic Temple, Wonder Bread Bakery, and the Detroit River, opened in 1953 as a complex of multi-story buildings and row houses.

There were two levels: three bedrooms and a bathroom on the second floor, and the kitchen with a dinette and living room on the first. Our basement housed our new washer, and I hung our clothes out to dry on the clothesline out back. There wasn't much to it, but it was ours, and we made the best out of what we had in that little home for our growing family.

Many Detroit residents from the Black Bottom area were eager to move into the new buildings. We were fortunate to be one of the first. A lot of respectable, proud, hardworking black families moved in afterwards. This was our first home without strangers or relatives. I could decorate it the way I wanted to for a change.

Detroit was now at a point of great transformation. During the mid-50s, the population in Detroit had reached 1.8 million. Streetcars were being phased out, and Mayor Albert Cobo was encouraging the push for the use of the new Department of Street Railways (DSR) buses, and also telling people to commute by way of the new freeways.

Occasionally, just for kicks, I would walk up to the corner of the new John C. Lodge Freeway and watch the drivers as they would exit. This scene really tickled me, because they'd often drive too fast and wind up having to slam on their breaks, causing their car to practically run into the easement. When that happened, their cars would slide back down into the freeway and they'd have to go through the entire process all over again. I took note, and learned from their recklessness. By the time we finally got a car, I was prepared.

CHAPTER 20

GIVE ME A HAND

We lived there in the Jeffries Projects in relative peace, from 1954 to 1958. It was really nice for me to have another female in our small apartment. Tab, who had been born a month before we moved to the Jeffries, balanced out our family of four. The boys loved her instantly.

On one occasion, when Tab was around age four, Wadean had gotten angry with me, but wound up taking his frustrations out on her. He was in such a rage that he pulled out his belt and began to beat her as if she were a man. This particular time, I chose to stand up to him. I was willing to die in order to save my baby.

I yelled, "Tab, go to your room!" and she quickly did as she was told. Next, I stood boldly in Wadean's path to her room. I said, "Beat me all you want, but you're not going to lay another hand on her!"

My firm stance stopped him in his tracks. To my amazement, Wadean didn't hit me, nor did he try to hit Tab again.

Afterwards, I went to the room where she was and found her still whimpering. I checked for wounds, and thankfully, there were none. Then, I sat and held her close to soothe away her bruised feelings and to let her know that I loved her and I would always be there for her. After a while, she fell asleep in my arms.

Today, if such a thing as that were to happen, the perpetrator would be thrown into jail and charged with child abuse. I suppose that ordeal with Tab caused Wadean to become aware, perhaps for the first time, that he was a father, that his children had feelings, and that they needed to be protected. Afterwards, I noticed a subtle change in him.

One day, while I was cooking dinner, Miguel came in to get a snack. All of a sudden, Miguel's sweater ignited into flames after he had gotten a little too close to the fire on the stove. Miguel flailed his arms helplessly in the air in an attempt to extinguish the flames. I reached to him and padded the fire out with my hands while trying to calm him down. Surprisingly, I did not get burned myself. I called for Wadean to come down, and he rushed Miguel to the hospital. We later found out that Miguel had suffered third-degree burns. I was horrified at the thought that I could have lost my child, but I was so thankful that Wadean was home for a change, and that he actually took Miguel to the hospital.

One summer I managed to convince Wadean to let me have a little "me time," and he agreed to watch the kids. Every Saturday I would get up extra early and get the kids fed, and then I'd be out the door. While out, I'd try to do as much as I could before I returned to the mundane lifestyle that I had found myself a prisoner of. I'd walk downtown to the Broadway Movie Theatre to see a western, and after that, a live show would follow. Back then those shows included acts from entertainers that we now consider famous. Dinah Washington was one of the performers I saw, and she was fantastic.

After the shows, I'd peek through the windows of the department stores and even grab a bite to eat as I made my way back home. It was such a blessing to be able to get away for a few hours, and just to imagine how things could be if my circumstances were different. I valued those Saturday breaks.

Every now and then, Wadean would show signs that he knew I did exist. I remember one time, I held a Stanley party, which was similar to a Tupperware party. I spent the entire morning preparing for a house full of guests, and by the end of the day, no one showed up. I cried my eyes out. This particular time, Wadean actually sympathized with me, and made me feel as if the evening weren't a total loss. Making friends in Detroit was difficult. I was a stay-at-home mom for the most part, and there was not a lot of socializing going on, especially since I was pregnant more often than not.

The year 1955 had rolled around, and this was a difficult time for me. I was pregnant again, and I was mostly irritable and uncomfortable the entire time. In May of that year, our daughter Dinah was born. With the addition of Dinah, we now had two girls and three boys.

I think that my sour mood affected Dinah during my pregnancy. Her temperament was odd, to say the least. She just wanted to be left alone. When she got older, I remember sending her and Tab out to play with the neighborhood kids, and a few moments later, she stormed right back into the house.

"*I don't wanna play* with them ol' ugly kids," she'd say.

I would respond, "Well, go on in there and look at TV then."

The older Dinah got, the less severe her feelings of isolation grew, but she still preferred to keep to herself.

As our family continued to grow, Wadean increased his time out in the streets, instead of spending quality time with his family. While Wadean continued to make new friends, I had a chance to catch up with an old childhood friend named Annamarie. She and I had been friends since we were kids. Annamarie was a little younger than I was. We reconnected after she and her husband moved their young family to Detroit.

Annamarie didn't live far from where we lived, and after work, she'd come over and prepare a meal out of my leftovers. Boy, could she cook! This went on for months, until I realized that my girlish figure had taken a turn for the worse. I had always worn a size 10, but after indulging in her reinvented meals, I blew up to a size 18. I couldn't stand it. But believe you me, I worked out during the entire summer, at the local gym up the street, to lose that weight. Before long, I was back to my regular size 10.

We were the second family to move into the new development. My neighbors, Jeff and Lillie Belle Samuel and their family, had arrived just before we did. We built a good friendship right from the start. We'd sit on the porch and talk about life, and comment on the new neighbors as they moved into our complex. We have remained good friends through the years, and we are still close. I don't know many people who could keep a friend for more than 60 years.

In January of 1957, our next baby was born. Rhoda (whom we nicknamed Ree for short) evened out our family, with three girls and three boys. At this time, the Jeffries Projects were just beginning to get bad in the neighborhood. But we stayed and tolerated it for awhile longer.

One time, shortly after I had Ree, I had gotten sick with the flu, and Wadean refused to help me in any way. Back then, the Projects had the old-fashioned furnaces that you'd have to shovel coal into in order to heat the house. With a new baby, I wasn't in any shape to take on such a strenuous activity. You would think that Wadean would have had no problem taking on that chore, but he wouldn't lift a finger. I just couldn't understand why he wouldn't do it. As a result, I ended up getting sick. To make matters worse, Wadean wouldn't even cook me something to eat whenever he prepared food for himself. He could be so cruel sometimes. The children and I suffered greatly because of that man's irresponsibility.

HOUSE 5:
THE HOUSE ON
PHILADELPHIA STREET

LOCATED RIGHT OFF of West Grand River, near the new Jeffries freeway, was the house on Philadelphia Street. It was a gorgeous colonial brick house with aluminum siding on the front. There were three bedrooms and two baths. All of the rooms were spacious. We even had two fireplaces.

One of the differences we noticed right away was that the entire neighborhood took pride in caring for their homes. Many of our neighbors planted flowers; so as to not be outdone, we did, too. There was a huge front yard and an even larger backyard.

There was a dry cleaner's on the corner, which still stands today. It had an ice cream parlor right next door. I made friends with Nancy Holton, who owned the ice cream parlor. The Holtons were one of the few white couples that remained in our predominately black neighborhood, and they were really nice to the kids and me.

One summer, Nancy would often close up the parlor early, and pick up the kids and me to join her and her two boys for a late-night picnic at Belle Isle. We had enjoyed ourselves so much, pretty soon, our picnics became one of our rituals. On some nights, if it were really hot out, we'd camp right out there on the beach. We would come home in the morning, with no hassles from Wadean whatsoever. For all I knew, he was out in the streets himself, having a grand ol' time. The craziest thing is, Wadean never had a problem with me socializing with white folks, but if I hung around Blacks, then *that* was a problem.

CHAPTER 21

WE BOUGHT A HOUSE

Wadean got a job as a sanitation worker. One day, while he was picking up the trash along his route, a speeding car hit him and broke his leg. The accident put a stop to his roaming the streets. Or at least it greatly reduced it. Having him home was quite different. He had matured over the years, and his temperament had begun to settle down somewhat. Wadean sued the driver and won, so we had a little extra money, for a change.

In 1958, with the extra money received from the lawsuit, Wadean decided he'd had enough of the Projects. That's when we bought the house on Philadelphia Street and finally moved out of our small apartment. The Eatmon clan was now settled securely in our fourth residence since Wadean and I had gotten married.

From the outside looking in, we were the perfect family. But *perfect* could hardly be the word used to describe what our family actually was. We now had six kids. I had never imagined that I would have such a large family. By that time, the older kids were able to pitch in and help take care of the younger ones.

Even though he still found time to carouse in the streets as often as he could, over the years, Wadean had become a bit more of a family man. He had become slightly more thoughtful of the kids. He even joined a men's club, which had a positive impact on him. The men in the group were very influential in Wadean's development as a man; they tried desperately to mentor him. They pushed him to be a better husband and father. For that, I was grateful.

Because we had so many kids and we didn't get out all that often, sometimes the kids would grow restless. In order to combat times such as these, we would try to come up with fun things to do in or around the house. On one such occasion, Wadean gathered the older boys, and they worked on projects that the entire family could enjoy.

One of their tasks was to install a portable swimming pool. During that summer, I found a job at a home goods store, so I wasn't home as much as I had been in the past. Needless to say, the kids all fell in love with that pool, especially the girls. They practically took up residence in the pool the entire summer. By the end of the summer, the girls' beautiful hair had turned to straw. I didn't know it at the time, but they would go swimming, and jump out and press each other's hair. I don't know who told them that it was alright to use the straightening comb on their hair, but they did it. It most assuredly was not alright, and their hair paid the price. In fact, their hair has never been the same since. By the end of the summer, I knew I had to come home, because everyone had gotten earaches, and the house had fallen into utter chaos.

Later that year, we decided to throw our first birthday party. Miguel was turning sixteen, and we wanted to do something nice for him. Since I worked at the home goods store, I was eligible to receive unemployment compensation when they laid me off.

With our finances fairly stable, Wadean and I planned to surprise Miguel. We were so happy to do it. When the day came, I told Wadean to pick him up from school. Wadean took Miguel to see his cousins; but while they were there, one of the girls asked if he was going to be at the party, so the cat was out of the bag. When the party started, Miguel came in and pretended to be surprised, but he later told us that someone had beat us to the punch and ruined our plans. Over all, we still had a good time.

Sometime later, Miguel began to come home from school with bruises, a swollen lip, or an occasional black eye. A couple of the boys from his class had started to bully him on a daily basis. This really got under my skin.

One particular day, Wadean told Miguel to take the garbage out, but he never came back. I sent Tab out to see what he was up to. She burst through the door shouting, "Diddee, Diddee! Some boys are outside beating up Miguel!"

Wadean shot out the door, and I followed after. There were two boys beating up on my boy in the alley, punching him in the stomach.

I told Wadean to do something. Wadean told the second boy, who was holding Miguel down, to let go; then he told Miguel to fight the boy who was the main bully. I have to admit, when Miguel stood up to that boy, he made me proud. Now I don't, in any way, condone violence, but I am a firm believer in defending yourself. I also believe in a fair fight. So when Miguel stood toe to toe with that little scoundrel and knocked his block off, I wanted to jump up and down in celebration. The boy got in a few good licks, but definitely, the fight was fair. Once it was all over, we called it a tie. And we never had any more bullying problems after that.

Wadean was on a roll. He kept the kids busy, as there was always some type of project or another going on. One winter, Wadean decided to build an ice skating rink. The kids loved that homemade rink just as much as they loved the swimming pool. Just like with the swimming pool, the ice skating rink was a major draw for the neighborhood kids.

One day, one of the neighborhood kids tried to do a skating move that didn't turn out right. Tab had just so happened to fall directly in the boy's path as he was coming down. He jumped up and landed on Tab's left-hand fingers, and practically severed her middle, ring, and pinky fingers. I looked out the window, and there was Wadean, picking

Tab up and bringing her in the house. I'm not sure why we didn't go to the hospital, but Tab's fingers were dangling from the thin pieces of flesh that still remained.

Wadean gathered all the kids together and pulled out the popsicles from the freezer.

"Come on kids! Hurry up and eat these popsicles. We need the sticks for Tab's fingers," he ordered.

Wadean suddenly became Dr. Eatmon on that day, in no time flat. He managed to calm all the crying children down, and mended Tab's fingers back together with popsicle sticks and duct tape. I have to admit, thanks to Wadean's quick thinking, Tab's hand healed just fine. She has been able to play the piano, pursue a career as a florist, and do anything else that she could think of that she wanted to do.

CHAPTER 22

COOKING WITH FIRE

Another spring rolled around, and my girls were as rambunctious as ever. Ree was still a little girl, but she was old enough to keep up with the older children and participate in their mischief.

One day I was in the kitchen preparing dinner, and Tab came in with a peculiar look on her face. "Mama," she said, "I think you better come up to our bedroom."

As I followed her up the stairs, the smell of something burning began to grow. I saw smoke billowing out from the girls' room, and panic seized my heart. The younger girls had built a tent, and decided it would be a good idea to make a campfire. After I quickly extinguished the fire, and I was finally able to calm down, I spanked their little heinies so they'd never try something like that again. Shoot, they could have burned the whole house down.

Over the years, Wadean's family had migrated to Detroit. His oldest sister Marlene sent for Ms. Katie to come join the rest of the family. Not long after Ms. Katie arrived, Marlene passed away. And Ms. Katie moved in with us.

One thing was for sure, her cooking skills had not been lost. Ms. Katie would bake the best homemade rolls you could have imagined. Not to mention her mouth-watering salmon croquettes. Late in the afternoon, the scent of her fresh-baked rolls would drift into the air, reminding me of the Wonder Bread Bakery not far from where we lived.

Like clockwork, our neighbor Cookie, who claimed that we were related, would come by with a fork in her hand. She would devour whatever it was we had prepared for dinner.

"How in the world does she know when to stop by?" Ms. Katie and I would jokingly ask each other. After a while, a bright idea hit me: I suggested to Ms. Katie that she start making her rolls in the morning. Cookie must have soon figured out that we couldn't take on another mouth to feed, because not long after Ms. Katie switched her baking schedule, Cookie's visits came to an abrupt end.

After a while, Wadean gave up on the men's group, deciding he no longer wanted to have anything to do with them. But just before he quit the group, they held a dinner dance, and Wadean actually asked me to go.

While getting dressed, Joe approached his father for attention. "Diddee. Diddee! Diddee!!" Joe kept calling out to his father, but Wadean continued to ignore him. Joe came back after some time had passed, and called out for him again, but after awhile, Wadean just shooed Joe away. After several more attempts, Joe left him alone. This behavior was typical of Wadean when it came to his children. It became so common that eventually even I began to ignore it myself.

When we arrived at the club, we looked and felt terrific. I was wearing a new dress, and Wadean was showing off his new tuxedo. You should have seen him riding up the escalator, as he propped his leg on the next highest step. He felt as proud as a peacock, strutting in his new suit.

When he reached the top, one of the other guests politely leaned over to Wadean, pointing and clearing his throat. "Hey man, your fly is open!"

Wadean was so embarrassed. After he zipped his pants back up, he whispered to me, "Now I know what Joe was trying to tell me." It took everything in me not to burst out into laughter. But because this was an important night for him, I managed to keep my composure.

Unfortunately, just when I'd think Wadean had settled down, the streets would call for his hasty return. I found out that he had a new stomping ground: he was going across the border to Windsor, Canada, to pursue his partying and philandering. One day Wadean brought two white women, Carol and Jane, into our home, claiming they were friends. I said to myself that he sure had his nerve; but I did not want to cause him to flip out on me, so I didn't say anything to him. Once I really got to know these ladies, they would visit on their own from time to time.

Eventually, I made friends with Jane. Carol, however, was a horse of a different color. I found her to be totally disrespectful. I remember smelling a putrid odor in the girls' room, and for the life of me, I could not pinpoint its source—until one day, I happened to be putting up the laundry and came across her stanky sweater hanging up in the closet. When I found it, I immediately threw it in the trash outside. Carol never missed it, never asked about it, and I never mentioned it, either. Jane, on the other hand, turned out to be a good friend.

Around this time, Wadean had a friend named Tom. Both he and Jane hit it off from the start. In fact, Tom and Jane wound up asking if Wadean and I would stand up at their wedding. The ceremony was to be held on the Ambassador Bridge. Tom was American and Jane was Canadian. They both thought that it was appropriate to marry on the dividing line between the two countries. Later on in our friendship, both Jane and Tom revealed that Wadean had often bad-mouthed me when I wasn't there. When they realized Wadean was a liar, they confessed that they were sorry for having misjudged me.

We didn't live that far from my Aunt Mary, whom we called A-Monk. She was a mentor to me. A-Monk introduced me to many different and exciting things in life. I actually joined the Birthday Club because of her. Not only were those parties an escape for me, but also they were loads of fun. Wadean didn't even mind when I'd host them at the house, either.

A-Monk enjoyed sewing. Back then, I had a great figure. A-Monk would make me beautiful dresses from time to time. One March, for my birthday, she made a black dress for me that hugged my curves in all the right places. It was backless, and so elegant. I looked great in it.

I loved those times with her, because she brought me those rare moments, when I would feel special. A-Monk was always thinking of new activities for me to do, or suggestions that she felt would enhance my life in one way or another. I was even invited to join the Eastern Stars, which is a Freemasonry-related fraternal organization open to both men and women. I was honored to be asked, but I decided I was not interested, thanked them for their hospitality, and gracefully bowed out.

Summertime had come and the boys began to find work. Joe was the first to show signs of being responsible. He went next door to the ice cream parlor, and started working immediately. The Holtons told him that they couldn't pay him, but he didn't care. I suppose he just wanted the responsibility of working somewhere, in any capacity.

While living on Philadelphia Street, I ended up visiting a local church called Nazareth Lutheran Church. I enjoyed attending Nazareth so much that I ended up officially joining. Wadean, on the other hand, never liked going to church. I can count on one hand the number of times he managed to attend. However, fortunately he never stopped me from taking the kids.

The church provided an escape for the kids and me. This was especially the case during the summer months. The church sponsored summer classes, dances, and bowling in its basement. This kept the kids busy, and since someone had to take them, I was right there along with them.

This was the longest I had ever gone without being pregnant. I thought that we were done with kids, but in February of 1960, our son Caleb was born.

We stayed on Philadelphia Street for another five years, until we lost that house due to foreclosure. Of course, Wadean blamed it all on me, but I don't see how it could have been my fault, since I never handled any of the bills.

The reality was that all good things must come to an end. If it were left up to me, I would have lived in that house for the rest of my days. Despite all that, at least while we were there, the kids had had a chance to continue to grow and come into their own.

Later, in mid-summer, we decided to take the girls down South to spend time with my parents while we prepared to move. One week had not gone by before we got the call that Tab had broken her leg. I made a mental note to myself about Tab. I had a feeling that this would not be the last time she'd break a leg; and indeed, it wasn't. Years later, after she had gotten married and had children of her own, Tab ended up breaking her leg again, while roller-skating.

HOUSE 6:
THE HOUSE ON VIRGINIA PARK

Tens of thousands of Southern Blacks moved to Michigan cities between the 1910s through the 1940s to escape rural poverty and win jobs in the world's most vibrant industrial economy, in Detroit. The Black Bottom Paradise Valley communities held many vibrant black middle-class entrepreneurs, professionals, retailers, and artists. However, in 1943, an unprecedented race riot erupted in Detroit, leaving 34 people killed, and requiring the presence of federal troops. For at least a decade to come, the plight of civil unrest continued to grow and heighten the flight of the white population from Detroit. By the mid-1950s, a growing exodus of employers also moved to cheaper land in the suburbs. To wreck havoc, the real estate industry began to practice red-lining, which denied Blacks equal opportunities for housing.—Craig Ruff, *Dome Magazine* contributor

EARLY ON, THE Virginia Park Historic District area was once regarded as an upper-middle-class community. In the fall of 1965, Wadean had managed to acquire a massive colonial revival home, about the size of a small mansion (with 17 rooms in total), which sat on the corner of Virginia Park and 12th. It was rumored that the infamous Purple Gang previously owned the house. But when we first moved in, it was a house that was desperately in need of help. At first sight, we all looked at each other in disbelief, and we wanted to run and hide, because it looked like a bomb had exploded in it.

The house was huge. It was a two-family flat, with two studio apartments. One was located in the basement and the other was located upstairs, adjacent to our attic. We worked from September 1965 till that November, to revive the ruins until we could call it our home. I remember the day we placed the final piece of the puzzle of this house back together. On that day, it was no longer an eyesore, but truly it was, at last, our beautiful home. We even planted a garden and placed flowerpots with assorted flowers on our porch to embellish our grand structure.

Among several other large homes on the block, our red brick house stood out, with its signature white-trimmed windows and a black roof. For accent, he installed a pair of heavy doors that we had painted white. Because the doors came from a church, when closed, the handles formed a huge cross, which we painted black. We all worked tirelessly to whip that house into shape. We painted; manicured the lawn and bushes; cleaned from the basement to the attic; and replaced the grimy old carpet that was there when we first moved in. The house on Virginia Park had come together so nicely in fact, that I could honestly say that I wouldn't have been the least bit hesitant to extend an invitation to Robert F. Kennedy, who drove right past our house while campaigning for president.

The moment we settled in, I had begun to feel bit out of sorts and decided to see the doctor. I received my diagnosis—I had hoped it was the flu. I had something all right, but it wasn't the flu. As it turned out, I was pregnant. I thought to myself, *Dang. Again*? I spoke to God and said, *Another child?* I had thought I was done. We had our last child in December of 1966, and named her Marie, whom we called by her middle name, Faye. Just like the rest of the kids, Faye was a bundle of joy.

CHAPTER 23

RACE RIOT

Now with eight children, living on Virginia Park, life was beginning to mellow out—at least, until the ongoing civil unrest had fueled yet another riot, which began in the summer of 1967. This time, President Lyndon B. Johnson sent the U.S. Army to assist the National Guard and the Detroit Police.

It was during this tumultuous time that I had to give all my fears to God, because I needed Him to ensure that my kids were safe. Once I checked the house and was sure that everything and everyone was in place, I handed the baby over to Dinah and ventured out on our patio to observe all the destruction that was taking place on 12th street.

Our city was burning up before my very eyes. The wind was so strong that it blew the fire onto our garage, burning the only good car we ever had. And the worst part is, the rioters threw rocks at the firemen to prevent them from putting out the fire. Once I saw the fire approaching our home, I thought, *Let me go get my babies.* But all of a sudden, the wind shifted, and the fire moved away from our house. The firemen returned with new hoses (since the others had been damaged by fire) and doused the flames that had consumed our garage. Fortunately, only the back of our house was scorched.

After the riot, the spirit of the people in the community had drastically changed. The riot had taken a huge toll on the black families on my block in particular. It seemed like everything and everyone around us began to break down. I was an eyewitness. Marriages began to suffer: men and women were at odds, separating left and right. Drugs and alcohol were running rampant, and you could just feel that times would get worse before they got better.

CHAPTER 24

TALENTS TO BLOSSOM

Despite the fact that we now had four beautiful girls and four handsome young boys, Wadean still never became the father that our children really needed. He was there physically, but he wasn't there emotionally, mentally, or even sociably in our lives. Positive encouragement from him towards the kids did not occur. Outside of a couple of family projects he created, he did not do any of the things a loving father would do with his children. As time passed by, life with him became progressively worse. I could truly see that Wadean's frustrations grew as he got older. He had come to the conclusion that he hadn't achieved anything with his life. He didn't care about any of his jobs; he had never been passionate about any of the tasks set before him.

Another thing that I believe contributed to Wadean's rapid decline was his wasted talent. He knew how to come up with innovative concepts and ideas, but he didn't know what to do with the things he had created. He didn't know anything about marketing, or patents, or about any of the tools he would need in order to be successful with his inventions.

Some of his projects were so far out, so far ahead of their time, people would ask, "Hey Walt, what in the heck is that, and what do you do with it?"

For instance, I saw the inline skates that he created. In fact, he sent a pair to the actor Gene Kelly, but since he did not receive a response, he became discouraged. Later on, I saw that same invention advertised in the mid-80s on TV. The sad part is, he had other talents—things he could do much better than most people. All of our children had the potential to be extremely successful as well, in whatever careers they chose to pursue. They all had tremendous talent.

Once, one of Miguel's childhood friends commented, "If you've ever heard of the Jackson 5, they could have been called The Eatmons."

And he was right. People loved to hear our children sing and play music.

One day, I invited a church member over for dinner. Wadean sat and talked with her, bragging about how talented our children were. Once she learned that the kids liked to sing, she was amazed. She had just recently made plans to move, and told Wadean that she wanted to give our family her piano because she had no room for it.

When the children found out that a piano was on the way, they were ecstatic. Miguel was the first to actually play the piano, and it sounded good. It was his singing ability that wound up opening doors for him. Once he realized that he was gifted musically, Miguel set in motion his plans to achieve his dreams. Opportunities would present themselves, including joining the dynamic group, the Dramatics; but for one reason or another, he would often be bombarded by life. Unfortunately, he had an ulcer that erupted, which brought an end to Miguel's aspirations for stardom. Nevertheless, Miguel did recover from his health issues, and he ended up singing with a group called The Gas Lights. They were a local group in Detroit that played small venues in the area. So Miguel did get to perform in front of live audiences for quite awhile. He was very creative too, constantly writing music and arranging his siblings in small groups to sing his songs.

David, who had a genuine love for music from the start, could play the piano like nobody's business. David had an ear for music; he knew when a song would be a hit. He kept me up to date with the latest songs, since he knew I loved to dance to the music of James Brown. He was the first one to introduce me to the music of Sly and the Family Stone, and to Stevie Wonder. David was less outgoing than my other children. I'd often catch him off on his own, perfecting his craft. Whenever he'd play the piano or sing, whoever was in the house would stop to listen. He could have easily been a concert pianist. In fact, his teacher came to the house one day, to ask permission to enroll David in a special school of performing arts. But Wadean denied the request. This disappointment not only crushed David's dreams, it crushed his spirit as well. I believe David's untapped strengths secretly intimidated his father. David wasn't afraid to share with the world his God-given talents. Wadean, on the other hand, was too afraid to share what lay dormant within him. Total opposites, there was always tension between them, and they never did see eye to eye.

Tab caught the music bug, too. She had a powerful voice packed into a tiny body. She picked up playing the piano just as fast as David. In fact, you could give Tab just about any type of instrument, and she would learn to play it in no time at all. She and her brothers really loved to make music together. Like David, Tab also had a teacher take an interest in her talent early on. That teacher's request was met with the same response from Wadean: a resounding *no*.

Wadean could be so hateful at times. He did his best to *discourage* his kids. With Motown Records, located just 7 blocks away from our house, my kids could have made it. By now they could have had a household name. But, despite their father's disapproval they let their voices be heard anyway, anywhere they could. I supported them as best I could, and I tried my best to see them perform wherever they were.

Tab had an opportunity to sing as a special guest on the radio. She was about 16 at the time. As nervous as she was, Tab sang her song like a pro, and it was a hit. Later, she joined a popular singing group at her school called The Troubadours. They were in such high demand that they sang at local venues all around our community. Once, I made arrangements to have them come and perform at our church; and I must say, it turned out to be one of my proudest moments. Any time my kids did anything that they were interested in, I'd find a way to be there for their performances.

Tab could perform modern dance, and sketch, as well. Once, she sketched a picture of a man, using only chalk. The colors in that drawing were so vivid that they would just pull you in, beckoning you to study every aspect of its composition. That picture was so good that Tab was able to sell it and make some extra money for herself.

Just before she sold it, I snapped a photo of it for a keepsake. Years later, the man who became her husband bore an uncanny resemblance to that picture she'd drawn. I always said that it was God's way of letting her know that He'd bless her with a man who would truly love and protect her. Today, they have been married for over 40 years.

The remaining children could not only sing well, but they also exhibited strengths in other areas. For instance, Joe had a mechanical way of thinking. There was a gas station across the alley from our house, and Joe worked as a service attendant there. It was there that he gained his extensive knowledge of cars. Joe loved to work with his hands, so his gift of tinkering with things opened doors for him. He later worked for Ford Motor Company. He took his time in everything he did. Although he was slow of speech, he did very well in his work. He was a sharp dresser too, always looking good. His love for nice cars made him stand out. Everyone loved being around him. He had a way of making anyone smile.

Dinah had a laugh that was hearty like my mother's. She was always the first on the dance floor. She would get up early in the morning, listening to the radio station WCHB, because she just had to hear her favorite jams while getting dressed for school.

One morning, I caught Dinah sneaking into our bedroom to get Faye. She loved singing to the baby. She explained that she just wanted to talk to her for a bit. Then she'd laugh it off. She would often say something that would have the whole house in stitches. Dinah also loved to cook for her brothers and sisters. Since we had a BBQ pit, when she would come home from school, she'd find anything she could to put on that grill.

Ree was a quiet and petite girl. She basically kept to herself. She had a favorite record called *Let the Little Girl Dance,* which she played so much that it almost made me sick. Eventually, I had to tell her to *let the little girl rest, or else*! On many occasions, I'd find her curled up with a book. It was her big sister Tab who greatly influenced Ree to begin reading books. She had a way of telling stories with dolls, which kept all the kids entertained for hours.

Ree looked after her little brother Caleb, and made sure he was safe. Caleb, who frequently suffered from severe nosebleeds, could always count on Ree to make sure the bleeding would stop. But it was Dinah who'd protected Ree when she needed it the most.

Caleb, the youngest boy, was just as talented as his brothers and sisters. He could sing and play the piano. In fact, as an adult, he wrote a hit song for the artist Millie Scott. Wadean didn't mind music and singing, so Caleb naturally followed the path laid out before him. Caleb was the only one who truly mastered the piano as an adult. But as a kid, he enjoyed just being a kid.

Caleb loved to follow behind his big brothers. Once, I caught Miguel literally throwing him down the hall. Caleb laughed as he flew passed me.

I yelled out, "Miguel! What are you doing with that boy?"

Miguel would say, "I'm bowling, Ma!" And then they'd both laugh till they turned blue in the face.

Caleb also had a sensitive side. I remember when the cowardly lion cried in the movie *The Wizard of Oz,* Caleb cried right along with him. He cried so much, I had to send him out of the room. Caleb was the type who wanted to try everything; but playing sports was not his strong suit. He must have had soft bones, because he'd break or sprain something any time he'd try out for whatever team interested him.

Our baby Faye was a happy baby. I would buy her toys from the proceeds of the Tupperware that I sold. What's more, the older kids would treat her like she was their baby. Joe always brought her gifts; and Tab, too. In fact, Tab would make little outfits for her. Faye still has a pair of pants that Tab made for her.

Faye was very shy, for some reason. Early on, I noticed Faye's temperament was not like the rest of my children. She was very sensitive. Wadean made everyone in the house so uncomfortable and on edge most of the time; I believe that this tense atmosphere affected her the most. But as she grew older, we discovered that she, too, was a singer. And she did it well. Her voice was very smooth and soothing. Whenever the mood hit her, she would sing out. I liked listening to her.

I believe that greatness starts when parents genuinely invest in their children. We are here to help them make their first steps, and guide them to their future. We are the ones who notice their unique talents before anyone else. A parent should never be in competition with a child. Parenting is work. It is your responsibility to make sure your child succeeds in life. They catch on so fast, and if we would take out the time to train them in the way they should go, when they are old they won't forget. This is a promise that God gave us.

But Wadean was ridiculous. He spent more time discouraging our children than speaking life to them. He really missed the mark in that regard. Our babies could have grown up to do even more than they did, to be even more of a blessing for many, and for generations to come.

As it was, on the bright side, our house was always full of music. Company would come over to be with our kids just because they were so entertaining. If you came to our house, you would get a concert. Or, we'd break out into an impromptu dance party. Singing from our children rang from our windows. In fact, people from the neighborhood would stand outside the window of the music room, and sing along with them!

Whenever my brother Lee came for a visit, he liked staying with us, calling it the highlight of his visit.

It seems that, despite himself, Wadean reaped the benefits of talented children, even without ever once pouring support, love, or patience into them.

Over the years, we settled in without fear of having to move anytime soon. And things went smoothly for a while. With the activities that we had created at the house, birthday parties, and random visits from cousins, life was turning out to be pretty normal. The kids were getting older, and I was fortunate to get good friends in my life.

Pat Johnson was another church-member friend of mine that Wadean didn't mind me going out with. She was quiet, and did not like to be around so many people. Since Nazareth consisted of many wealthy families, some of who were snobs, Pat took a liking to me. One day after the service, she said, "Come with me, Mary. I'm going to teach you about culture." Starting that day, every Sunday that summer, I would go somewhere new and exciting with her: the Cranbrook Institute of Science, the Detroit Symphony, or the ballet. I basically went anywhere that she could think of where I would be exposed to class and culture. I learned a lot about life, and the finer things life has to offer. Pat was a true blessing to me. I didn't know it at the time, but later, when I became a single parent, these excursions helped me to expose Faye to some of those same things so that I could better help guide her through life.

CHAPTER 25

UNNECESSARY CRUELTY

At this stage in his life, Wadean had his highs and his lows. During the high times, he would engage with the kids by dancing, joking, and taking them on family outings. He had the kind of laugh that would ring throughout the house. But, during his low times, the mood of the entire house would change for the worse. Back then, there wasn't a name for what he suffered from, but I believe that today experts would have diagnosed him with bipolar disorder—a brain disorder that's also called manic depression. People with bipolar disorder experience unusually intense emotional states called "mood episodes." An overly joyful or overexcited state is called a manic episode, and an extremely sad or hopeless state is called a depressive episode. Sometimes, a mood episode can include both, called a mixed state. People with bipolar disorder may be explosive and irritable during a mood episode. Bipolar disorder can be treated, and people with this illness can lead full and productive lives; but in those days, we knew nothing about it.

As a child, Wadean was raised with no restraints or boundaries. And when children grow up with no guidelines, they will end up being like a bull in a china shop.

In our case, we never knew when that bull would show up. There would be long periods when we'd live in peace. During those times, the kids felt free; I felt free. But then the tide would change, and that's when we lived with a bully.

At times, Wadean's treatment of us all was tolerable. At the very minimum, he did provide for his family financially; but in the areas of love, affection, compassion, and leading by example, he certainly fell short. He had cut down on hitting the streets, and resorted to "fishing" instead—or so he says—but I know that he was still out with other women. He and one of his buddies made this a weekly adventure; we loved it when Wadean was gone. This went on for years.

Wadean was a hard taskmaster. With this style of parenting, our kids did not have the opportunity to live their young lives to the fullest. It did not always sit well with him to see his children enjoying themselves. He took pleasure in watching them work all day and into the night. This was a daily ritual.

It is ironic that he worked them like this, since he never followed any of the rules that his mother had set when he was a child. Truly, it is very fortunate that he had the most respectful kids a parent could ask for. To this day they have maintained the same level of respect around me as they did when they were under his roof.

It really was a toxic life we lived through. I should have acted much sooner. I, too, became complacent, and was under the impression that I would not make it on my own.

Over the years, Wadean's inner struggles continued to fester, and the frustrations he suffered from would cause him to lash out. He was, overall, a tyrant.

It seemed that the girls suffered more than the boys, unfortunately. He would take them down to the Red Light District, in his attempt at teaching them about whores. Another time, Wadean actually had the audacity to teach them about dikes. That was too much. They were too young for those types of lessons. On top of that, he didn't want them to socialize with boys at all. Wadean would accuse them of having sex, when I knew for an absolute fact that they were not.

He had gotten so bad that I decided to confront him about it. "What is your problem, Wadean?" I asked him. "Is it that you want them all for yourself? What, I'm not enough for you?"

He glared at me as if he wanted to wring my neck, and then he turned and walked away without a word. Because of the circumstances surrounding our first encounter, by the time I was twenty, I was considered too old for his particular taste, so I knew I had to keep a close watch on my girls.

Chapter 26

Gone Fishing

Back in November of 1966, when I was in my third trimester with our daughter Faye, the call came in that Wadean's mother had died. We rushed over to his niece's house, where Ms. Katie had been staying. When we made it to her bedroom, I immediately turned around and went right back out. Seeing her in that condition didn't sit well with me. She literally looked as if she had seen the devil himself. As I waited in the hall for Wadean to say his last good-bye, I saw him lean over to kiss her on the cheek. When he stood up, it was as if another man had emerged. From that moment, his demeanor went from bad to worse.

As months went by since Ms. Katie's passing, Wadean became increasingly more sinister. Ordinary everyday housework had become an exercise in futility, because in Wadean's eyes, we could do nothing right. It had gotten to the point where if we heard the screen door shut, everyone inside would cringe. The children would jump instantly and grab a broom, a rag, or whatever, and start cleaning, even if the house was already spotless. One day, I looked up and saw Dinah rubbing a clean wall with a dry rag, and Wadean actually smiled. It was as if he had to see work of any sort, period, being done at all times, no matter what it was, what time it was, or who was doing it. I remember one of the neighborhood girls made the comment that whenever she would visit our house, she would pick up a broom too, just so she could stay without any issues. He had them doing crazy things, like painting the tree out on the patio, or sweeping the alley. He even had us hauling trash in a dump truck. His requests had no limits.

One day, early in the morning, right after Wadean had left for his fishing trip, I woke up all the kids and decided to take them out.

They whined, "Awe Ma, why do we have to get up so early, if Diddee ain't even here?"

I told them that we were going hiking, and told them to just be quiet and get dressed. They resisted that idea at first. But, once I got my coffee and fed them, we were ready to hit the trails. I only wanted to walk for a couple of hours that day, but they liked it so much, we wound up staying out on that trail until it got dark.

On another occasion when Wadean was preparing for a fishing trip, this time he picked up on the fact that the kids were looking forward to his absence. I had gone so far as to tell them to keep their excitement hidden from him, for fear of him lashing out. But Wadean was very observant. When he realized that his fishing outings were more joyous for us than they were for him, he sat his fishing pole down and told us that because we took pleasure in his leaving, he wasn't going fishing anymore. The short breaks we enjoyed had come to an end.

Any time when he was gone, it was as if the warden had granted furloughs to his prisoners. Now, with his increased presence, he also became more accusatory towards us. The conclusions that he would come up with, in his mind, validated his right to beat the kids and to terrorize me.

CHAPTER 27

ACCOUNTS OF ERRATIC BEHAVIOR

Evidence of Wadean's erratic behavior could easily be found in his mistreatment of any one of us. He continued to wreck havoc on our lives.

Miguel:

- One day Wadean sat Miguel in a chair all day and tried to force him to read (at the age of four), with no success. He scared the boy with his browbeating and whippings more than he taught him.

- As a young man Miguel seemed to have had a closer bond with his father more than any of the other kids. But, one day, Wadean turned on him and grabbed Miguel by his collar and belt and literally tossed him out of the house, where he landed on the seat of his pants. To this day, I still don't know what transpired for that to take place.

- Miguel decided he wanted to marry a young lady from around the corner. I couldn't help but think about when I got married, and how lonely I was. I had hopes of vindicating myself by having the entire Eatmon brood show up to celebrate their big brother's marriage. Since Miguel had eloped Wadean refused to allow any of us to attend the reception. I myself resisted and went, anyway. When I returned from the reception, I was forced to bear witness to the tears that ran down my kids' faces, as they were busily sweeping the patio and painting bricks at nighttime. I truly believe Wadean found pleasure in making everyone around him miserable.

Joe:

- Joe was extremely sensitive, so his heart was easily bruised; yet Wadean repeatedly tore Joe's character to shreds. Just because Joe suffered from a slight speech impediment didn't mean that he was stupid. But Wadean was constantly abusive when Joe talked, saying things like, "You's a dumb, dumb, dumb, dumb ...dummy!" Joe's self-esteem was severely damaged.

- As an adult, Wadean taught Joe to drown his sorrows in vodka and orange juice. After a couple of failed marriages, and many of life's disappointments, Joe grew more depressed. The older he got, the more his troubles contributed to his early demise.

David:

- When David was in his late teens, Wadean jumped on him, daring him to fight back. He knew that David's eyes were very weak, almost to the point of being legally blind. I believe he wanted to injure his son's eyes in order to ruin his sight permanently.

- Wadean kicked him out of the house, and entirely too early. David wasn't quite ready for the world. He was very mild-mannered. To be pushed into the streets with no type of preparation was very irresponsible on Wadean's part.

- Wadean chose the most inopportune times to humiliate David, no matter who was around. Even when David was an adult, Wadean belittled him in any way possible. But the most hurtful was when he introduced David to his friends as his *thang*, or even worse, as his *daughter*.

- Once, when David told Wadean that someone had molested him, Wadean seemed to condone it.

- After Wadean had gotten older, David tried to help him out around his house, due to the fact that he had been issued hoarding violations by the City of Detroit. David organized everything; but then Wadean attempted to have David arrested for stealing his things. Fortunately, the police said that they would not follow through with the arrest. David was done dealing with his father from then on.

Tab:

- After Tab got her first job working at Cunningham Drug Store as a waitress, Wadean asked her to bring back a bag of beans. Tab said okay, but added that it wouldn't be until later. Then she said, "too bad, I won't be able to eat any of them." We don't know why she said that, but for whatever reason, Wadean totally misunderstood what she said, and went berserk. Later on that day, he walked into the store cursing and shouting at her while she worked. When the manager stepped in, Wadean let him have it, too. Needless to say, she lost that job.

- Then Wadean humiliated her when it was time for prom, by accusing her of using her prom as an excuse for her to have sex with her date. He refused to buy her a prom dress. Thanks to Madea's help, Tab was able to go after all, in a beautiful dress with matching shoes.

- On Tab's first trip home from college, Wadean banned her from the house because she rode home with a young man from school (whom she later married). Tab fled to David's house for refuge, and Wadean followed her. He jumped on her. Tab yelled out as she covered her face, while he kicked, slapped, and punched her, basically trying to kill her. It was David's feisty little wife who jumped in and helped rescue Tab.

Dinah:

- Wadean molested Dinah when she was little, creating in her a warped feeling of acceptance. As she grew older, he then resorted to rejecting her and humiliating her. This crushed her young spirit, and greatly lowered her self-esteem.

- On another occasion, he spied on Dinah as she entered a neighbor's house. We didn't know it at the time, but we found out later that he would often use binoculars to spy on all the kids as they went to and fro in the neighborhood. Dinah hadn't been in the house that long before she heard her father on their porch yelling, "*Dinah! Dinah!* If you don't get yo' black ass out of that house, *I'm going to tear you in half.*" Next, he burst into those people's home, almost knocking their door off its hinges. He caused Dinah to bolt from room to room, and when he caught her, he literally ripped the leg off of one of their beds, and began to beat her with it; he continued chasing her down the street until they reached our house.

- During Wadean's last years, after he had had major surgery, it was Dinah who reached out to care for him. As a reward, he slandered her name, telling every family member that she was greedy and only after his money, when in actuality she had asked only for a little money to help with the utilities.

Ree:

- Dinah stood up to Wadean for the sake of Ree: Dinah saved her when she once walked in on him pulling Ree's panties down while she weakly cried out, "But *Diddee*! I'm a good girl...I'm a good girl!"

- He knew that Ree was a timid fifteen-year-old. Dinah tried her best to protect her from him. Even though Ree kicked and screamed, and Dinah tried with all her might to make him stop, he'd push Dinah so hard that she'd fall on her bottom. Each time he knocked her down, it caused her to emotionally lose her confidence, which was then replaced by rejection. Dinah literally put herself between him and Ree, telling him, "*Naw Diddee*, you *ain't* gonna do this!" Eventually, It was Ree who stopped Dinah from being further attacked, by saying, "Dinah, just let him get it over with." Despite Dinah's efforts to shield Ree from the molestation, he penetrated two of his large fingers inside her, three agonizing times, saying, "See, Dinah, I need to make sure she's still a virgin." I believe that it was his intention to personally take their virginity before either girl could go to her first high school dance.

CHAPTER 28

WE'VE HAD ENOUGH

After some time had passed, Wadean's temper seemed to have reached a boiling point. That's when I made the decision to leave Wadean for good. But before I left, I found out that for some reason, Wadean had taken my name off of our joint bank account. This left me with no money whatsoever. So I took another job.

Wadean must have felt rich. I began to notice that he was spending money with both hands, as if it would never run out. There was only one outcome to his dangerous new financial trend. He eventually emptied that account, and then came after me.

Earlier that day, I went to work at Miller middle school in the cafeteria, serving the students. When I returned home, I was exhausted. I hadn't even had time to change out of my uniform. The only people in the house were Dinah, Ree, Caleb, and Faye. I made my way to the kitchen in order to prepare dinner for the day. The children were each doing their own thing in different parts of the house. I can still hear the random notes being played by Faye as she pecked on the piano in the music room.

All of a sudden I heard Wadean storm into the house, shouting obscenities. While I was at the kitchen sink, he grabbed me and accused me of stealing his money. I didn't even have a chance to explain to him that there was no way possible for me to have done what he accusing me of, because I no longer had access to his account. He dragged me into the dining room and proceeded to move our dining room table over to one side. I knew this was bad.

With all the commotion, the older kids came storming into the room. I had prayed that Faye would continue to peck on the keys so that she wouldn't see me become a punching bag. Wadean was so big; I would not have made it.

I looked at my babies who were all in the room, and they were horrified. They were helpless. They were just as small as I was.

But this time they had had enough.

Wadean, still ranting while moving the table, started calling out my name. He flat out said that he was going to kill me that day. I felt like a child waiting for my whoopin.'

I looked over at my kids; tears were streaming down their faces. They had never seen Wadean beat me. We all were scared. Thank God, Faye stayed in the music room.

He said, "*Give* me my money, Mary."

I said, "I don't have it."

Smack...right across the face.

Dinah yelled out before I could, "Diddee, *No!*"

I don't know if I was sobbing for myself, or because of what my children had just witnessed.

Again, he roared, "Give me my *money*, Mary!"

"I don't have it," was my meek reply.

This time, he punched me so hard, I fell to the floor. My arm hit the small table where I kept all my houseplants. It was at this point where everything went into slow motion. *Oh no*, I thought. *I don't hear Faye playing the piano anymore. Oh God, she's coming in here.*

The next thing I know, he yanked me up by my right arm, and Faye was in the living room screaming her head off. By that time, he had pulled me to my feet, and Dinah, Caleb, and Ree went to work, trying to save their mama. Caleb was so small, but he jumped on Wadean's back. He looked more like the cape on Superman rather than Superman himself. But I could tell that the grip that he got had choked his father something good, because it distracted Wadean from me just enough. The three of them were fighting their father as if their lives depended on it. And they were probably right.

This gave me the chance I needed to run to my nightstand. I remembered that he had bought me a .22-caliber gun for protection. I was so nervous, I could barely hold the thing properly. I didn't want to make a mistake and hurt my kids, but I had to take this opportunity. As I ran back, I could hear him cussing my kids out, and they were giving him a rough time, too. But I knew that after a while, he would grow tired of yelling and start to hurt them next.

Years ago, Wadean had been kicked out of Kronk Boxing Gym because he didn't fight fair. He wasn't sparring the right way with those men; instead, he had been beating them to the point of death.

I knew I needed to hurry with the gun.

As soon as he saw me, he snatched my arm, saying, "Gimme that—" and he quickly turned the gun on me.

My babies' eyes were as wide as the moon. Their mouths dropped open. They rushed to my side. Faye stood frozen in that one place crying her heart out.

Wadean called out to Caleb, "Take Faye upstairs to Mrs. Rankins."

My heart sank. I didn't know if I'd ever see Faye or Caleb ever again. He didn't even let me hug them. But I had my big girls with me. They positioned themselves in front of me like shields.

With every word he yelled, my girls shouted louder and louder: "*Don't shoot*, Diddee! Don't shoot! *Please...don't!*" He yanked me by my arm, and shoved me towards the bedroom; but just then, Caleb came back.

"Come on in here, boy!" Wadean exclaimed, as he shut the door.

Meanwhile, Mrs. Rankins could hear our screams. Once she heard us shouting the words that rang the loudest among the others—"*Don't shoot!*"—she jumped on the phone and called Tab.

Wadean clenched tightly to my arm with his left hand, and with the gun in his right hand, he directed the kids to stand against the same wall where the bed was. He made them stand there with their arms raised, as if they were thieves caught by the police. I was truly helpless. He raised the gun to my head as he ranted on. Just then, Faye burst through the door.

At six years of age, her mere presence shattered the moment. Wadean told Caleb, "Get her out of here!"

This allowed Wadean to regroup. He was rattled.

As soon as Caleb had returned and reached his spot, we heard a voice on the other side of the door. It was Tab. She yelled, "*Hey*! You've got *five seconds* to let 'em out of that room, *or I'm going to blow yo' head off!*"

Wadean, in a loud whisper, ordered me to tell her to leave.

So, I said, as calmly as I could, "Tab, honey, please go. We don't want no trouble."

She yelled right back in a more stern tone, "Heck *naw*! I ain't going *nowhere*! Diddee, I ain't playin'. You've got *five seconds* to *open this door*!" As she said this, she struck her husband Bill's shotgun against the door. When she did that, we all jumped.

She yelled like a madwoman, "Let 'em out *now*!" At the time, she was 6 months pregnant; I guess her temperament had changed.

This was the last thing I wanted. She had her entire life ahead of her. She was married now, and to drag Bill into this was wrong.

I could feel Wadean's grip loosen. At that moment, hope took over my heart. He leaned down again and ordered me what to say to her.

"*Tab!*" I yelled. "He said he'll let us go if you leave!"

"*No—*" she yelled. "Send them out *now*! *One*! *Two*!"

Then the other kids were yelling all at once, "Tab, *please*, wait! He promises to let us go if you would just leave!"

She finally agreed, but not without her last statement: "*Alright*! *I'll leave.* But I'm not going far. Everybody! *Pack your things*! I'll be back."

CHAPTER 29

KIDS: PACK YOUR THINGS

After Tab left, without saying another word, Wadean left. Then, with bold conviction, I told the kids, "Pack only enough clothes in order to change." Next, I called Wadean's niece to come pick us up and take us over to Tab's house, which she agreed to do with no hesitation. And that was the very last time I stepped foot in Wadean's house. It couldn't have come any sooner.

As a city worker, Wadean would earn a living, yet he'd take the money and use it for frivolous things just for himself. We needed things: clothes, school supplies, food, etc. But he would rather throw money out the window than manage it the right way, to benefit his family.

He was so neglectful that he never bought me much, either. He didn't even buy me a wedding ring until the last two years of our marriage. Over the years, I had begun losing my teeth. Wadean did buy me some partials, but even those were short-lived. On one occasion, our girls were getting bigger so he bought all of us a coat. I needed one most of all. Other than that, I had to shop where I could.

On the other hand, Wadean would help his other relatives without the slightest bit of hesitation, even before he spent money on me and the kids. He could be so incredibly irresponsible. He had one niece (the child of his half sister) who wanted to take opera lessons, and he paid for them. To this day, I've yet to see her in concert or to purchase an album. The funny thing is, she may not have even known that he did this. When she got married, he gave her away, but she wouldn't allow us to attend, nor did she allow him to see the pictures.

Wadean told so many lies about me to his side of the family, many of them hated me for years. At least until he died, and some even afterwards. And these were the same people that I had grown up with. I know they saw how badly he treated me; yet in their case, blood was thicker than water. I learned quickly to let them go. But I still love them.

It's been 27 years, and Wadean never really showed true kindness towards me. I never knew what it's like to be loved by a man. We never shared special secrets, as a man and his wife would in a normal relationship. We were not close at all. You can look at photos of me around the house, and see that on most of them, I never smiled.

Wadean worked me like a slave. He had me drive dump trucks and other commercial vehicles, which he'd bring home. I had to carry heavy things, far beyond what a woman my size should ever have to carry. I was made to cook whatever type of wild game or fish he felt like eating. And by the time I turned 41, my hands looked as if they belonged to an 80-year-old. He was too cheap to buy new pots for me to cook in; he'd find old ones on his garbage routes, and I'd have to scrub them clean.

Nevertheless, all of that made me a strong woman. It was what I needed to fuel me for where I was headed.

HOUSE 7:
THE HOUSE ON MEYERS STREET

FOR A PERIOD of 18 months, we lived with Tab and her husband Bill. They had moved into a three-bedroom and one-and-a-half-bath brick colonial, with a big bay window. It had once been property that Nazareth Lutheran Church owned, and Tab and Bill had been able to move in with no problem.

The house sat in the middle of the block, with a maple tree in the back. Tab and Bill didn't have much, but when they painted the rooms, the colors that they chose made it feel like home. I had never seen an orange dining room before, but somehow it worked. It was a nice transition into the den, which was all wood-paneled.

This was the first time that we had a garbage disposal, and even a milk chute. Although we didn't actually have any milk delivered, that chute played a huge role in our lives one day when we were locked out of the house. We didn't know what to do, until we looked down and saw Faye. She was just the right size. So we put her through that chute, and she got in and unlocked the door.

CHAPTER 30

TURNING OVER A NEW LEAF

By February 1973, Miguel, Joe, and David were all married, with their own families. Since we had no other place to go, we were still living with Tab and her husband.

After that gun incident, I finally knew that it was no longer safe to remain under the same roof with that man. Bill and Tab were more than understanding about my situation. So much so, I could have just cried because of the emotions that overtook me.

Even though they had not too long ago gotten married themselves, they accepted us into their home with no problem, nor with any hint of hesitation. I had told them up front, that if they weren't able to let me stay with them long enough so that I could get back on my feet, then they might as well leave me where I was. I said I would take my chances and hope that I would still be living by the time the rest of the kids were old enough to live on their own. But Tab and Bill would have none of that. They assured me that I would be fine, and that my kids would be, too. It was a bit crowded for a while, but we made the best of it.

As I said, Tab was pregnant when we arrived. She had been feeling sick during this time, so we stepped right in to help her and Bill. I cooked and did the budget, and my other girls cleaned. Meanwhile, I continued to work in the school's cafeteria, not knowing yet what I'd do during the summer.

We made the best out of our situation while staying there. I remember one Saturday morning I was staring out of the kitchen window at the kids playing near the maple tree. That tree brought me a sense of peace. I almost felt as if I lived in another city.

When I first moved in with Tab and Bill, I had very little, but they shared whatever they had with me. While staying there, I continued to maintain as much as possible the routine that the kids were used to: luckily, the older girls were able to attend their same school, since Tab lived in their school district.

But one day, Wadean was lurking around the front of their school, like some psycho on the prowl for new victims. He was determined to force me to come back to him, and I was just as determined *not* to. During that time, I would take them to school and pick them up. I thank God that Dinah spotted her father out there in front of the school, and had enough wisdom to call me at Tab's to let me know. I immediately made a beeline up to the school. I told Dinah to get Ree and meet me in the back of the school.

When Wadean realized that we had blocked him from taking the kids, he resorted to full-fledged threats. From then on, if anyone ever left the house for any reason, those who stayed behind would run to the front window to watch as that person faded away down the street. Basically, by this time, Wadean had become a stalker. He would park at the end of the block in hopes of catching one of the younger kids, or me, off guard.

Wadean had become increasingly enraged over the fact that we had left him. He blamed Tab for it. But there was one problem: the truth is, he was a coward. I don't know why, but it's a fact: he would not cross the line that Tab had drawn. Whenever he would call the house to harass me, Tab would be on the other phone listening to make sure that she would be ready to interrupt his plans.

CHAPTER 31

AN UNPLEASANT SURPRISE

One Sunday morning, he called, and as usual, Tab was on the other phone listening in.

Wadean said, "*Tab?* Can't I talk to my wife privately?"

She answered, "This is *my* phone!"

At that point, Wadean did not bite his tongue. He cursed me out, and proceeded to tell me that if I didn't return my wedding ring, plus all of the girls' new coats, any of the clothes and underwear that he ever bought me, and the partials in my mouth as well, then he would come to our house and bust me in my mouth and snatch them out.

I told him that it was not necessary to hurt me, and I said that he could pick everything up by noon.

Before we hung up, Tab, in total disbelief and utter disgust, defended me, belting out, "You said you want her *teeth? Really?* Well, come on over here, and *get* them! You *better* not try anything when you get here, *or else.* You *hear me?*"

Needless to say, Wadean hung up on her. Tab was my special gift from God. She was my Lone Ranger. I must have looked like I was paralyzed, because after I gathered all those items, and pulled the teeth out of my mouth, all I could do next was flop back on my bed.

I watched Tab stomp through the house in a rage. *"Mama! Get* me some hangers!"

She took as many hangers as she could find, and hung every single item designated to give back to Wadean. When he arrived, he pulled up to the house and saw on the porch everything that you could think of, hanging for all to see, including my panties. I think he was more embarrassed than I was. She even had sanitary napkins hanging there on a hanger.

He later called and asked, "Why would you do *that?*"

At that point, Wadean had it out for Tab, vowing to pay her back for what he called "ruining his family."

Tab sure fixed him. She later said, "Mama, don't worry about your teeth, and whatever else he gave you. We'll buy you whatever you need."

He actually thought that he had accomplished something. He went about bragging to his family and friends about what he had done.

I later learned that all of them told him, "Wadean, you' a fool. No one deserves to be treated the way you treated Mary."

One day, after that ordeal, I must have been in deep thought, because Ree walked up to me and asked, "Mama, you're not thinking about *going back*, are you?"

I told her, "*No*, I would never jeopardize our family's well-being by returning to your father."

Dinah was strong, as well as smart. Out of all the problems that she had dealt with at home, she still managed to graduate on time. I am sure it was Dinah's determination that saw her through it all.

Dinah once said, before we moved from Virginia Park, "Mama, when I turn 18 and graduate, I'm leaving."

I agreed, even though I didn't want her to leave just yet. I knew that Wadean had ridden her way too much. He tried with all his might to wear her spirit down, but Dinah was too smart for that.

After Dinah graduated that summer, I began working as a summer coordinator at Nazareth Lutheran Church. That year they had extra money, so I was able to get paid for that. This allowed me to save towards our daily needs. Working at the church was good for me. It took my mind off of my problems. I had about 50 youngsters to plan activities for. I'd take Caleb and Faye with me, to keep them active as well.

Since I worked constantly, the activities of my older kids were left to themselves to manage. At first, Dinah and Ree felt that they were grown up enough to stay out all night. But after I got out my rod of correction, they quickly calmed down. Then Dinah got a job at the Paramount Bar.

Raising the girls was not easy. One evening a call came in that a car packed with six men was chasing Dinah, with intentions of raping her. But she kicked and screamed so loud that the people came out of their houses and helped out, and chased them away. By the time she made it to the house of one of her brothers, she was shaken up, but I managed to calm her down.

Unfortunately, Ree later developed the art of sneaking off. Out of the blue, by the time she had reached 17, she had met a man who turned out to be just as mean and hateful as her father. He took full advantage of my girl's naïveté. Just like me, when she lost her virginity she was not ready for the world. We had just left from under Wadean's cruelty when Ree decided to take matters into her own hands. Her new boyfriend had managed to persuade my daughter to marry him.

Ree knew that I would not give her my consent, so she went back to her father—the same man who had assaulted her a couple of years earlier. I knew, from personal experience, the consequences of getting married at an early age. I didn't want Ree to travel down the same path that I had.

Of course, Wadean approved the marriage, and I was furious. He knew that this would hurt me deeply, and that is probably what convinced him to allow it.

To make matters worse, Wadean did not come to Ree's rescue when he walked in on her husband as he was about to punch her in the face. In fact, after making eye contact, he signaled to him not to hit her in the face, but somewhere else on her body instead.

Ree is still not able to talk about the despicable things that her husband did to her, to this day. When I finally did find out about it, I nearly fainted. But when she did eventually get away from him, she managed to remarry: she found a very kind man who vowed to take care of her—for well over 20 years now.

After Ree left home, Dinah still insisted that she was leaving, too. My family was beginning to shrink before my eyes.

It took about 18 months, but I was finally able to move out of Tab's house. We stayed on Meyers from the spring of 1973 through the fall of 1974. During that time, I experienced many trials. Life for me was moving so fast, I could barely catch my breath; but I knew that the Lord was there to assist me, because I truly needed help. It was His strength that helped me find my path in life.

Before I decided to leave that godforsaken marriage, I had prayed to the Lord. I did not realize that I was actually making a covenant at that time. In my prayer, I told the Lord that I was going to leave. I vowed to step out, counting on His word, and trusting in Him only. After I made my commitment to the Lord, I knew that He heard my plea, and He answered my prayers.

CHAPTER 32

WOMEN'S RIGHTS

B y 1973, the Affirmative Action Movement had picked up steam and was gaining momentum. I was pulled along for the ride.

Early in the spring, I received the best news in the world: jobs were beginning to open up, and I had been offered a chance to choose one of two positions from two different companies. The best part of all is that I also heard that they were specifically looking for minorities, and for women in particular. They were both paying the same rate, and the interview for each was to take place at the same time. All I had to do was pick one. I figured it wouldn't hurt to apply, because money was in short supply for me.

I made my choice. My application was accepted, and then I was hired. I received my first permanent job working for the City of Detroit's Department of Street Railways (DSR), now known as the Department of Transportation (DOT). Before I could actually take the job, I had to pass all of the required tests and complete eight grueling weeks of training. When it was all said and done, I became one of the first of seven black female bus drivers in the history of the City of Detroit.

I can vividly recall all the stares I'd get when I first started driving that year. People would be in shock to see a female bus driver. In those days, most people just assumed that women were not capable of handling a vehicle that big; but they didn't know that Wadean had prepared me years ago.

Believe it or not, many men were reluctant to board my bus. Some skeptical passengers would actually step back down out of my bus when they saw who was behind the wheel. Still others would gawk with wide eyes. I would politely welcome them. "Good morning," I said, with a big smile on my face. "Step right up, please." My motto was, *A bus driver should be patient, courteous, and cheerful.* This was just the beginning of a whole lot of firsts for me.

In 1979, I was one of three women to be promoted to Transportation Station Work (TSW). Then, in 1981, I was promoted to Transportation Terminal Assistant (TTA).

One of my most cherished achievements came in 1983, when I was promoted to Transportation Emergency Dispatcher (TED). All of the positions I held while working at the DOT were predominately held by males. As you can imagine, the atmosphere in the office was sometimes quite volatile, especially back in those times. There were many instances when things got too rough at work, and I had to speak up about it. During those days, I was determined to maintain my femininity as well as my sense of identity. Truly, I am grateful to have gone through all of the trials I went through, because I believe had it not been for brave women such as myself, who were willing to step up to the plate and challenge the status quo, the advancement of women and minorities might have taken even longer to get off the ground and running.

I did extremely well while employed at the DOT. The Lord was with me all the way. It seemed like as soon as I got there, it was as if they had been waiting for me with open arms. I went from one promotion to the next, with little to no opposition.

So many positive things were happening to me, as a matter of fact, some of my co-workers were saying, "It's a *miracle*, what's going on with Mary."

I would say, "It sure is, but this ain't *my* miracle, it's *God's*."

I was able to work for the DOT for 20 long years, full time, and I don't regret one minute of it.

I went from barely getting by and struggling just to put food on the table, to $12,000 annually in 1973. I know that may not sound like a lot of money in this day and age, but back then this was nothing short of a great accomplishment for me. That salary would actually be worth over five times that nowadays.

I was a single parent in the 70s and 80s, and I didn't need my ex-husband for anything. Becoming one of Detroit's first black female bus drivers was no small feat. And that is something I will cherish as long as I live.

I made some really good friends along the way, too—friends I am still in contact with. Shortly after I started my new career as a bus driver, I managed to catch a ride with various co-workers. Jackie was one of them. We were hired in at the same time. Jackie was 16 years younger than I was, but that made no difference to her, and she still helped me. To this day, she and I are friends.

Back then, your name and your integrity really meant something. And I learned that when a woman carried herself in a certain way, men respected her.

People honestly wanted to help me. Everyone on the job knew that I needed a car, so both men and women always made sure that I had a way to get to work. One day one of my co-workers approached me about helping me to get to work. He had a brand new Cadillac, and didn't mind sharing it with me. He told me that he'd pick me up in the evenings so that I could take him to work, and then in the mornings when my shift started, I would drive in and switch as he got off.

This worked out just fine, until I was able to get a piece of a car for $50. And boy, that thang was something else. I always had to carry a gallon jug of water, because it had a leaky radiator and I didn't want the car to overheat. It didn't even have windshield wipers or heat, and no defrost. But for awhile, it got me from point A to point B.

After about six months, another co-worker was generous enough to co-sign a loan for me, and I was able to get my first brand new car. It was a light blue 1974 Ford Pinto. This was another sign that things were looking up and turning around in my favor.

CHAPTER 33

CAREER WOMAN

While I'd been living with Tab and Bill, I still had to get used to this new job, driving the bus. But I had made up my mind that I could do it, no matter what. I had never been more determined. The required eight weeks of training were hard. I had so much to learn and memorize. That was truly a stressful time for me. But with Caleb and Faye enrolled in their new schools, I was able to focus on training on the road.

Fall was a beautiful time of the year, and a great time to learn the routes and how to properly maneuver a bus. I have to admit that this was not my first time driving large vehicles. As I mentioned, Wadean had a fetish for commercial vehicles, so he had made me drive them from time to time. You never really know just how God will prepare you. God will always make you ready for what comes your way.

During my training period, I had several instructors, each of whom had their own unique way of training. I was determined to master the art of driving, no matter who trained me. During my final session, the inspector I had couldn't find anything to criticize me for. The only thing he managed to alert me on was that my sweater was hung on the back of my seat instead of on the hook above my head. I thought to myself, *big deal*.

The new drivers were assigned certain routes for a set period of time. One time, in particular, I had the Hamilton run. The driver nicknamed "Wire-head" partnered up with me at Northland Mall, picking up passengers at every other stop. One day, he thought that he could outsmart me. He would follow me from Seven Mile and the Lodge Freeway in an empty bus. He thought that it was funny to watch me pick up all of the passengers that the driver before me left, including his passengers too. This went on for approximately two weeks; that entire time, I felt bewildered.

Wire-head would also ride my bumper with no one on his bus. He thought it was funny. At the end of the run, he'd drive past me, laughing hysterically. But one day I got him back.

As usual, I'd pick up my passengers, but on this occasion, I took my time. My first stop was normal, but instead of pulling off, I waited a few moments. Adjusting my transfers, straightening my clothes, I did whatever it took to waste some time. I checked my side mirror and saw that my strategy had not phased Wire-head one bit.

At the next stop, I did the same thing, and looked out my side view mirror again. This time, I could tell that he was beginning to flinch. I could see him checking his watch and peering through the windows, trying to figure out why I was falling so far behind schedule.

By the time I got to my third stop, he had run out of time. My passengers began to figure out what I was doing, and they began to laugh. They had seen how frustrated I had been in recent weeks. But I did this to teach him a lesson. I was late, as usual, and I had to go to the restroom, but it was all worth it. By the time I made it to my fourth stop, you should have seen him. He got so nervous that he pulled out from behind me and jumped in front of me to make up his time.

That day, I did to him just as he had done to me. I rode his bumper. And whenever he went into a bus stop I would go right in with him, bumper to bumper.

Ol' Wire-head never messed with me again after that. The next day, he became my partner and *helped* me with the passengers, instead of making my runs more difficult.

Things that I would have never have imagined took place. I had grown comfortable with the stares I received. Some were pleasant and some were not. I remember one time when I was driving the Hamilton Line, I was at a stoplight, and two young ladies who were crossing the street looked directly at me, and each one gave me the Black Power fist and shouted out, "Right on, sista!" They were so excited for me that I burst out laughing as I drove off in pride. They really made me feel good.

I'd always pull up to a bus stop with a big smile. Many would greet me with a smile just as big as mine, but some of the male passengers would snub me and say, "A *lady* driver? What is the world coming to? I'll wait for the next bus."

These men would not board the bus simply because a woman was driving. They claimed that I had taken their job. And I'd shoot back, "If this was your job, then you would be driving and not me; and I am not about to feel bad for having a good-paying job."

My passengers and I grew fond of each other, for the most part. However, there were a few who had proven themselves to be unpredictable. One time, there was an old drunkard who boarded the bus and acted very foolishly towards me. For some reason, he wanted to pick on me; but after a while he settled down. Later, after he had gotten off the bus, my female passengers told me that they were all set to snatch his arms off and beat him with them if he'd tried anything.

I have sat through fights, and dealt with some of the rudest people you could ever imagine. The night runs were the scariest. But it didn't get deep until one time a troublemaker got on the bus. He was a young white man who seemed nice. He even picked up some of the trash off the floor. He paid, and went to his seat. After a few stops, a young black man boarded the bus. He needed change, but I couldn't do that, so I told him that he should ask the other passengers. As he was walking, the young white man must have said something bad, because the black man suddenly beat him to a pulp. I continued to drive, but I did call for help. All of a sudden, the black guy got off, and the white guy remained.

After a while, everyone got off one by one, except for the white guy. I was thinking to myself, *Oh boy, I smell trouble.* I said, "Sir, you are going to have to get off."

"No I don't," he replied. "I can ride until the end of the line." And that's exactly what he did. At that point, it was going on midnight, and I was getting nervous. But just before I reached the end of the line, he went to the door to get off. Right before I could breathe a sigh of relief, he decided to put his foot between the doors so that I couldn't close it and drive off.

I didn't know what he had planned. Yet as he began to speak, my nervousness subsided, because I realized all he wanted to do was apologize to me for causing the fight. He stood there with a bloody nose, disgusted with himself, embarrassed. He did apologize, and I was much obliged.

Many people objected to my position, but I proved them wrong; I did my job well. The DOT had "spotters" (undercover personnel) who rode the bus, observed the driver, and reported back to the department. Every report that was submitted about me had rave reviews. On top of that, many of my passengers sent in commendations to say what a good and courteous driver I was.

HOUSE 8:
THE HOUSE ON TULLER STREET

IT WAS NOVEMBER of 1974 when I was finally able to purchase my own house. It was a small white bungalow with aluminum siding. It had three bedrooms: two downstairs, and the third was a finished attic. I even had a nice-sized basement. Faye's and my room were both located on the first floor. During the summer months, we'd sit on the sun porch, which was adjacent to her room, and enjoy the breeze. On extremely hot days, we'd relax and even sleep out there. During the rest of the year, my family and friends mostly gathered in our combined kitchen/dining room.

This area was the main hub of the house, since the house was so small. This was the first house I lived in where I truly experienced peace and quiet. On the other hand, my experience as a new homeowner was not exactly what I had anticipated. I remember after signing the documents for the house, the realtor seemed to have a problem giving me the keys.

As I moved in, I quickly realized why he had taken such a long time to give me those keys. The first night that I pulled into my driveway and opened the side door, I was surprised when I entered the kitchen, looked over where the sink was supposed to have been, and saw that there was no countertop, nor was there a sink. The only thing there that was actually installed were the cabinets. I dropped everything I held in my hands, and rushed through my new house. All of it looked normal, until I reached the bathroom: that shyster had taken all the bathroom fixtures, too. The only fixtures that remained in the entire house were the bathtub and the utility sink, located in the basement. That first night, my heart was broken. We had no place to use the bathroom.

The next day, I called the realtor and told him that we didn't have a toilet, and no sinks. I told him that if he didn't replace the missing fixtures and the countertop, I would call the housing authority and report him. It took a week for him to respond, but he did finally install all new (although much cheaper) fixtures.

Several months after the reinstallation, I still had to replace the fixtures myself. To make matters worse, one night we came home and the house was full of black smoke; it smelled like something had been burning. I told Caleb and Faye to wait on the porch while I went in to check. To my great relief, the house was not hot. As I walked over towards the entrance to the basement, I could hear the furnace humming. I called Detroit Edison, and they sent their inspector over. He explained that the furnace was old, and that it had at least 26 code violations. He then disconnected everything that tied into the furnace. He told me to call the realtor and have them replace the furnace, because certainly they already knew that it was bad from the beginning.

It was clear that the realtor had hoped that I wouldn't find out until after the first year had passed. This was due to the fact that after a year, according to the contract, the responsibility of any repairs on the furnace would have been on me. But again, I told him that I would report him if he didn't replace that old decrepit furnace. He immediately sent someone over to replace the furnace with a brand new one. To this day, that furnace is still working.

I set to work to make the best of that house. I bought furniture and decorated it the way I wanted. I kept the walls white and installed carpet throughout the house. It was perfect for me. I even had a garage.

Mr. and Mrs. Bell were good neighbors. They watched out for Faye and me. Mr. Bell ended up being my handyman. He kept my lawn looking immaculate. He'd even paint whenever I needed it.

Just when I thought I could call my house my "home sweet home," I suffered from a series of break-ins. The neighborhood was not the best. The neighbors were quickly turning into ruthless thieves. I ended up installing iron gates on all of the first-level windows. At times I just couldn't catch a break. I was still fairly new on the job and learning new procedures; and keeping up with my kids and maintaining a new home required a lot of mental and physical effort. But I did it, and I survived.

Even though the house on Tuller Street was not my first choice, I knew that I really needed to settle down. I made the best of it, and ended up living happily in that house for 20 years.

CHAPTER 34

NEAR-DEATH EXPERIENCE

During the beginning of my second year on the job, a man boarded the bus, coughing nonstop. He coughed so much that he coughed right in my face. I looked at him and realized that he was really sick, and he looked frail. I didn't think anything about it after that day.

Over the next few months, I continued to drive, but someone commented that I was sick and didn't know it. I looked malnourished. Come to find out, I was sick indeed. In fact, I was ill to the point of death. I had just returned from a trip to Las Vegas with friends, and while I was there, I noticed that I was extremely tired. I had also experienced an abnormal amount of weight loss.

It wasn't until I had returned to work that I finally said to myself, while I was driving my route, *I need to go to the doctor.* It seems as though as soon as I thought that, the dry cough started. Around that same time, I admitted myself into the hospital to have a hysterectomy; I had fibroids that I needed to get rid of. Right at the beginning of the procedure, the doctor stopped, and immediately closed me right back up.

He told me that if he had continued, I would have died right there on the table. I was so full of infection that there was nothing he could do. Come to find out, I had genital tuberculosis. I didn't know it at the time, but when you have the tuberculosis virus in your body, it can end up in your reproductive organs. I wound up spending a large amount of time in William Beaumont hospital.

Fortunately, because I thought I'd be recuperating from that operation, I had already sent Faye to stay with my parents in Birmingham, and Caleb was staying with his father. So, I didn't have to worry about who would care for them. In the meantime, since I had complications, Madea and Daddy went ahead and enrolled Faye in my old school back home in Alabama, Councill Elementary School.

Madea called her sister, Martha, in Pittsburgh, and asked her to come to Detroit. Once Martha arrived, she immediately called Madea, telling her that things were worse than what I had led them to believe. The doctor informed my family that I did not have long to live. By the time Madea arrived, I was in total quarantine. I didn't realize that my own children knew more about my condition than I did. They tried to be strong, but I knew something was wrong.

They all crammed into my room, but once the nurse came in, she kicked everyone out. David attempted in vain to hide in my closet. The kids were all so funny as they tried to hide behind the curtains, under my bed, and in my bathroom. I guess they held themselves together pretty well, at least until Madea came. After that, it seemed that things began to unravel.

Tab was pregnant with her second baby, so she was stressed out. The last thing I wanted was for her to get sick again. During her first delivery she had had five seizures in the middle of pushing her baby out. I took her illness hard, as I did with any of my kids' problems, when I happened to find out about them. I remember that at that time it seemed to me that they all were falling apart.

The kids told me that Wadean was up to no good, as I had expected. He thought that it was fitting to add salt to my wounds. He knew that I was sick, so it looked like he wanted to finish me off. From what I was told, Wadean waited until Madea returned with Faye, and then he took a simple conversation and manipulated Faye's comments in order to keep her from going back to Birmingham with Madea.

Just as the family was leaving to come to the hospital to see me, he showed up at my house to take full custody of Faye (who was eight years old at the time). Everyone was crying, horrified at what he'd do if he didn't get his way. But Madea convinced him to allow her to take Faye to the hospital so that my youngest daughter could see me one last time.

I remember watching the monitor: I saw Faye and my grandkids. They were all crammed in one chair, giggling away, saying, "Hi, Mama! Hi, Grandma!" It was really good to see them.

You know, as I think about it now, the doctor never once told me how bad off I really was. Once everyone arrived, I could tell they were really stressed out. The tension in the room was so thick you could cut it with a knife. They were starting to bicker and fight amongst themselves. I did not like that at all. I later found out that Dinah had taken my illness the hardest. Earlier in the day, Tab told Dinah that crying couldn't solve anything, but Dinah told her that she had a right to feel the way she did. Dinah cried so much, though, it put everyone on edge.

Thank the Lord, once it had been confirmed that Wadean had taken Faye, I miraculously decided to be healed. For another three weeks, I stayed in the hospital and started on the mend. With all that I went through, I never got the operation that I had originally gone in for. I survived without ever having the hysterectomy.

CHAPTER 35

CLEAN BILL OF HEALTH

It took months for me to recover from the tuberculosis, but I finally did. When I went back for my follow-up appointment, the doctor was ecstatic. He took me by the hand and pranced me throughout his office, telling the staff that I was a living miracle. He had never told me that I was dying—until I was healed and returned for that follow-up visit. He went on to tell the staff that he wouldn't have given two cents for my life when I first came to him.

Once I got my clean bill of health, the first thing on my agenda was to find an attorney who would help me get full custody of Faye. Unfortunately, the first attorney I hired was a crook. He thought that he was slick enough to burn both ends of the candle by representing *both* Wadean and me. He thought that since I was a recipient of the affirmative action movement, which allowed me to work a city job, that he could not only help Wadean gain custody of Faye but also get him child support.

Well, I sure fixed him. I went out and hired a Jewish attorney with a stellar reputation. I had to laugh, because on the day of the trial, after everyone saw who my attorney was, Wadean's attorney just got up and moved to drop the case—all before we even reached our seats! It took about a year to prepare, but in less than five minutes, I was able to take Faye by the hand. We walked out of the courtroom for good, together.

Once I finally got Faye back, she looked jaundiced, and her hair had fallen out. I should have told her to leave everything she had back at his house. Sadly, it seems as though she had brought in a bag with roaches in it. My house quickly became infested.

No matter what we tried, we could not get rid of those pests, until eventually I tracked down a new serum to get rid of them, and that finally did the trick. I soon found rest in my home again.

On the whole, I actually had more good days in that house than bad.

CHAPTER 36

A GRAND OL' TIME

In the spring of 1977, I bought my first luxury car. It was an all-white Grand Prix. Back then, I felt like I was driving a Cadillac. One day, as I drove the kids to school, people everywhere were tooting their horns and shouting out cheers to me. I laughed when I pulled up to the intersection and heard a young girl yell out, "*Ooh-wee*! Look at that white car! Go 'head, mama!" Life for me had finally leveled out.

Several years later, I remember throwing myself a 50th birthday party. I felt free to invite anyone I wanted to, because Wadean was not around to influence my guest list. Each year I felt stronger. I wanted to take life by the horns. I even started dating.

I took my first Caribbean cruise. I visited Miguel while he was stationed in Germany and the surrounding countries, for an entire month. I visited Mexico, and many other countries. On many of my trips, I traveled alone, but I still enjoyed myself.

Here in the United States, my favorite place to visit was New Orleans, where I took my parents for their anniversary. I also saw many other sites that our nation had to offer. I guess my proudest moments were when I was able to plan family trips, especially our trip to Washington, D.C. And, I even visited The White House.

I was having a grand ol' time in my life. I tried a little bit of everything, including arts and crafts, riding snowmobiles, and even skating. I made that a weekly activity, with a neighbor's child and my family. I became very active, and I enjoyed every minute of it. I was even good with the high-impact aerobics, and sometimes I would lead the class at the local gym. On occasion, I would rent a cabin on the shores across from Mackinac Island, and take Faye and Caleb.

I loved the arts. Any time a good concert would come to town, I'd take Faye. We'd get dressed up and just go. It didn't matter where. One of our favorite pastimes was our visit to the Detroit Institute of Arts to have *Brunch with Bach*. This was a big benefit to Faye. When I got her back from her father, I had seen symptoms of withdrawal. She slept constantly. It felt to me like she was slipping away. I really believe that with her father she had suffered from some sort of emotional trauma. So whatever I had to do in order to keep her from regressing, I did it.

Faye had become so shy. You couldn't even give her a compliment without her bursting out into tears. As a teen, I actually asked her, as I stared deep into her eyes, "Faye, are you in there?" I knew that if I didn't do something quick, she would be lost.

Every day, she became more and more distant and withdrawn. She was tall and felt awkward, which didn't help. She had become irritable around my grandkids. She just wanted to be left alone. I attempted to counter her self-imposed seclusion by indulging her every whim. Whatever she wanted to do, I hung in there with her. I had to work, but I was still able to keep a close watch on her and let her do whatever I thought would help promote emotional growth.

When she was 12, I enrolled her at the YWCA, for swimming and gymnastics. Then we tried modeling at the age of 13; but she wasn't ready for that just yet. Posing in the window at Montgomery Ward's Department Store was too much.

One day, when she was 16, Faye found a flyer at a festival, and said she wanted to try modeling again; so I let her. This time, she was ready. I watched her blossom into a young lady right before my very eyes. She still had to make some adjustments with regard to her temperament, but now I knew that time would take care of that.

Every morning, I had her check in at the office of her school, because I still didn't trust Wadean. There were many uncertainties that affected her: changing so many schools in such a short timeframe; her brutish father; and me being sick. These things weighed a lot on her. But we got through it together.

During all these years, I had done a lot. But I still wanted more in life. So, in 1980, I decided to go back to school and get my GED. I am glad to say that I finally got my High School Diploma. From there, success was in my future.

Later, in my fifties, I was introduced to the sport of square dancing. I met so many people who participated in this dance, it actually gave me energy. I was very privileged to dance with people who were in their nineties. I still find the time and the energy to dance today.

Everything I missed out on in my youth, God certainly did redeem it all for me. And just when I thought that life couldn't get any better, the Lord began to place a call on my heart to teach His word. I began to take my time with the Lord more seriously, so I decided to increase my studies. My appetite for His word began to grow. I felt so encouraged that I wanted to tell everyone about the goodness of God, and how He was able to provide for and to protect me and my children.

I began to teach the mid-day Bible study at church. For a short time, I'd even have some of my grandchildren over for weekly Bible study, which later branched out into my own radio show, which lasted for one season.

That experience led to another radio program, where I was one of the prayer counselors. Once, I took a listener's call who was at the point of suicide. (Out of respect for this person's privacy, I can't go into detail about her issues.) I was able to encourage this individual, and after many months of counseling, she recovered, and we have actually remained friends for over 20 years.

Whenever I went home to Birmingham, Daddy would ask me to teach there as well. That brought a lot of joy to me, knowing that my father approved of me after all the things I had gone through. I didn't know it then, but I was being groomed for greatness.

Our family time evolved into annual events. One of our all-time favorite activities during the summer was the annual family breakfast. They liked it so much, that breakfast lasted into lunch, and eventually into dinner. The kids, and their families and friends, even from other cities, faithfully came every time for this event.

During the holidays, our house seemed to expand. I'd prepare a mouth-watering dinner, and my family would fill the house. I wasn't able to buy gifts, but I'd cook, and bring everyone together. They couldn't wait to eat my famous turkey, and oyster dressing, and macaroni and cheese, with all of the other sides, to fill a plate. But then, some of my in-laws would come and cart off the remainder of my food. I guess they thought, since the food was packaged up for my sons, what was the harm? Well, I bet you guessed it: I quickly put a stop to that.

CHAPTER 37

GENERATIONAL CURSE

My children, who had all been abused in one form or another by the very same man who helped bring them into this world, eventually shared with me the atrocious wrongdoings they had suffered while we were with Wadean. He had also turned his prurient interests to some of his own grandchildren.

Tab and her father had an estranged relationship. However, just before Tab had totally written her father off, she received a phone call that he had passed out on his front porch and that she should go and check on him. So she and Bill, along with their two daughters, Tyra and Kristen, went over to the house on Virginia Park to visit Wadean. They discovered that gout had overtaken him, and as a result, he had really let the house go. The place was infested everywhere with rats, roaches, and trash. When they saw her ailing father living in squalor, they chose compassion, and took pity on him. They extended an invitation for him to come live with them; Wadean quickly accepted.

Sometime after Wadean moved in, he soon realized that the girls were heavy sleepers, so he began fondling his youngest granddaughter.

Both Tyra (13 years old) and Kristen (11 years old) had their own bedrooms. Since Tyra was a teenager, no one ever thought that he would stoop so low as to touch the youngest girl, at his age. Well, we were wrong about that. In fact, he would attack Kristen in her sleep. Until one night she woke up and realized what he was doing. He took her little frame and held her by the neck, and began choking her, raising her up off the floor. He threatened her, telling her that if she ever told anyone what was going on, he would kill everyone else in the house. To top it off, he even showed her his guns to prove that he meant business. He had accomplished his goal: to get back at Tab for "ruining his family."

I truly believe that because of Wadean's sick and sadistic tendencies, Tyra rushed into marriage too soon, at the age of only 16. Unbeknownst to any of us, Wadean had allowed Tyra to meet up with a 21-year-old man who would eventually get her pregnant. One day, out of the blue, my daughter Dinah found out that Kristen had been hanging out late at night. When we confronted Kristen about it, both she and Tyra broke down and admitted that it was because of their grandfather. Dinah then called a family meeting at Tab's house. The audience began to grow, while their father sat, eavesdropping, in the other room.

Dinah exposed the whole ordeal: how Tyra hooked up with her husband, and why Kristen was beginning to act out of character. When confronting Tyra's husband, for getting her pregnant, he put all the attention on his new bride's grandfather, Wadean. He explained that it was Wadean who had told Tyra she could continue to meet with him to have sex, while Wadean patiently waited for her in the car outside of her boyfriend's house.

Next, the focus shifted to Kristen: he said that she was being fast, and that she, too, had a boyfriend.

Tab turned to Kristen and asked, "Are you still a virgin or not?"

"I don't know. Why don't you ask your father?" Kristen replied boldly.

Dinah said that she was confused, because Wadean had told her that Kristen was a dike—that she actually liked other girls. At that point, both Tyra and Kristen were sobbing uncontrollably. Tab and Bill were stunned, rendered speechless by what they were hearing.

Bill broke the silence. He rose up, and called Wadean from his hiding place. When asked why he had done all this to their babies, Wadean's excuse for violating Kristen was, "I was trying to make sure that she was still a virgin, because, Bill and Tab, you just don't know how to raise your girls properly."

It was at this point that Tab snapped. She rushed down to the basement, and returned with the same gun that she and Bill had intended to use to rescue us at the house on Virginia Park. She tossed the gun to Bill, and ordered her husband to kill her father.

"He's not worth it, baby," said Bill. "Plus, I ain't about to be separated from my family to go to no jail."

Thank God, Bill was able to calm down and think things through logically.

As a result of her traumatic ordeal, Kristen soon suffered from several meltdowns. Her first episode occurred in the car with her mother. One day, she and Tab were on their way to the store. For no reason at all, she began babbling, saying that she couldn't sleep; that she wouldn't sleep; and nobody knows that she'll never be able to go to sleep. Then she proceeded to yell at the top of her lungs.

Through intervention and lots of prayer, Kristen was able to battle her demons. But the damage she and her sister received at the hands of their own grandfather affects them to this very day.

Bill was a God-fearing man, a man of character. It took all the restraint in heaven and on earth for him not to take matters into his own hands once he found out about his father-in-law's incestuous acts. He later told Tab that he felt utterly helpless over the fact that he could achieve no redemption for the wrongs that Wadean had inflicted upon his children.

I found comfort, however, in the fact that Bill didn't go to jail. I was so relieved that he hadn't carried out his wife's request to kill that monster—the man I'd married.

Keep in mind: back then, the laws were not as stringent as they are now concerning molestation and child abuse. Had the consequences of the law been in place then as they are now, Wadean would surely have gotten what he deserved.

CHAPTER 38

WE MUSTN'T FORGET THE LAST TWO

The way I figure it, Wadean must have concluded that since he had been able to cause a world of pain and disappointment on the majority of his older kids, why not mete out the same type of aggravation on the last two? Somehow, his sick mind desired to inflict abuse on each person in the family; he didn't want to overlook anyone.

Caleb:

- Just before Caleb turned 18, I found out that he had met an older woman with a child, got engaged, and then married her in less than three months. Wadean knew that this, too, would hurt me, as he signed the papers to approve that union. The boy just wasn't ready. Ten years later, he left that woman, and moved as far away from Detroit as he could, and stayed away for at least 20 years. His father may not have physically abused him then, but I know for sure that Wadean knew the consequences of marrying a woman who was much older than he was, and how the adverse effects of that decision were going to play out in his young life.

Faye:

- When Faye was 20, Wadean accused her of stealing money from him. When Tab and Bill decided to take a family vacation in California, Wadean and Faye went with them. While there, someone asked if she had any spending money, and she said that she had brought four hundred dollars. He overheard their conversation and stewed about it for weeks afterwards. After the trip, he confronted her, and when she tried to explain that he had misheard, because she took only the usual hundred dollars that he normally allowed her to have, and that it was her own money that she had worked for and saved up herself, he didn't believe her, and jumped on her.

He cursed her out, as if she were a man, and then proceeded to choke her. This time, however, he was older, and so was Faye. She was able to fight back pretty well. They fought in Tab's dining room, overturning the table and leaving broken glasses and dishes everywhere.

This hurt Tab beyond words, because it reminded her of what he had done to her at that age. Tab was helpless to stop the fight, since she had broken her ankle at the time; the cast was fitted up her entire leg, so her movement was extremely limited. However, Tab's daughters were there. They were still young, but they were there to help defend their aunt Faye.

Ironically, this was the same thing he had accused me of. Wadean never paid any attention to how he wasted his own money, yet he didn't mind constantly accusing someone else of stealing it.

- Wadean racked up plenty of offenses with Faye. He put her through enough emotional roller coasters to last a lifetime. The last straw came the day he called to tell her that he was eligible for Social Security, but left it up to her to ask his estranged second wife to split the money, allotted for his children, with her newborn baby, who was carrying the Eatmon name. The only problem is, Faye had just turned age 18; and that baby did not actually belong to Wadean. His second wife was well along in her pregnancy when they met, and he took her and her family in as his. This broke Faye's heart. She loved her dad, but he had chosen, as usual, to extend his help outside of his own family. Needless to say, his wife said no. Faye needed help at the time with her last year in high school and with going to college. She missed every senior event, because I didn't have the money to help her. Had it not been for the Lord, she would not have made it through college. Boy, Wadean could be so despicable at times.

HOUSE 9:
HOME AT LAST

OVER THE SPAN of two decades, I watched my neighborhood become run down. I could tell that if I didn't prepare for the future, I could very well end up being stuck on that block until I died. It took me approximately five years, but I got my finances in order and paid off my bills. Once the neighborhood had reached the breaking point, where I didn't care to put up with it anymore, I moved. *Thank You, Jesus!*

Finally, in 1993, through prayer, the Lord said to me that it was time for me to retire. I had purchased a new car and was blessed enough to be able to pay that off in full within the first year. Next, He allowed me to purchase my dream house, located in downtown Detroit, about a mile away from the Detroit River. It was a tri-level with a two-car garage, and all the amenities that a condo would have, yet it was a co-op. I was able to pay that off too, and have only the monthly assessment fee to worry about.

It has wall-to-wall mirrors and a galley kitchen on the main level. My bedroom and the family room are on the second level, while Faye's bedroom and the main bath are located on the third level; I even have a powder room and a finished basement, with a separate laundry room. We also have two patios, one with a finished deck. This house is everything I ever dreamed of. I retired the right way, with God's many blessings.

CHAPTER 39

MINISTRY IN MOTION

Once I moved in and had gotten settled, I was able to focus on my education. In 1995, I started college, and later I graduated with a bachelor's degree in Christian Counseling/Biblical Studies. When the time came for me to graduate, I had the opportunity to travel to Greece and Egypt for my Senior Project. That was an awesome opportunity, and definitely a blessing from God.

Soon after, I was able to help others through Christian Counseling; I worked specifically with married couples, and I was able to minister to young women who needed to define who they were in God. Shortly afterwards, I was ordained as a licensed minister, giving me the greatest feeling of accomplishment.

Later, I took on the role of a manager at a women's transitional home. The ladies there would take my guidance as I helped them make it through their trials. They understood that what I taught was just common-sense advice based upon my own experience, enhanced by the Word of God.

Then I decided to start my own ministry. I got some business cards together, and called it Ministry in Motion. My slogan was, *Have Bible...Will Travel.* This was a big leap of faith, but I put my trust in God every step of the way.

Next thing I know, I was getting calls to come teach small classes. By this time, I was certainly prepared for it. I was spending a lot of time in Birmingham, caring for my aging parents in conjunction with a church down there under their "Watch Care" ministry. The pastor there asked me to teach on a regular basis. I laughed, because he knew that I lived in Detroit; but he was willing to wait until I'd visit, which was often.

Back home in Detroit, I was asked to teach an in-home monthly Sunday Bible Study for close friends, who were all meeting in honor of a loved one who had gone home to be with the Lord. It wasn't long before they chose me to be their regular speaker.

After that, I got word from a former church that they wanted me to continue to do their mid-day Bible Study on Tuesday afternoons. I accepted the task, and, after eleven years, I am still faithfully teaching that class.

After one of my square dance associates became ill and moved to an assisted living home, while I was visiting, I asked the owner if it would be okay for me to start a Bible Study class. She said yes. I started to go there weekly to minister the word of God.

Later, the owner told me that she had opened an adult day care center, and she asked me to minister there, too. This is a great joy, because I love being with people and bringing them the Word of God.

Finally, someone at my current church overheard that I had an evangelical ministry, and they recommended me to become an associate minister. After I worked with my pastor, I was accepted on the ministerial alliance team. I now manage five ministries! Although I never remarried, I am very glad and fortunate that God chose me to do His will.

Instead of complaining about the woes that life dished out to me, I chose to change any negatives into positives. At age 83, my life is still full, and I desire to do even more. I believe that writing this book will allow me to continue to encourage more people around the world who are seeking to know the healing and saving grace of Jesus Christ.

Outside of the wisdom that God has blessed me with, I garnered additional habits of good conduct over the years, which have evolved from the valuable information I learned from my brief membership in the Girl Reserves. There, I memorized our motto, in which each letter stands for the following positive attributes:

Gracious in manner
Impartial in judgment
Ready for service
Loyal to friends

Reaching toward the best
Earnest in purpose
Seeing the beautiful
Eager for knowledge
Reverent to God
Victorious over self
Ever dependable
Sincere at all times

I hope that as you have read through this book, you will be inspired to follow the above practice in your everyday life, as I have, and turn your life around for the better. God is in your heart, and He will always guide you.

EPILOGUE

When I was young, I thought that I would get married to a great man, and we would have a wonderful family. But perfect dreams don't always come true. In fact, the route to success and happiness may come through a journey of many years of suffering.

When I revealed my secret after 65 years, I found that the accounts of my story released others, too, from their burden of secrecy—specifically my children—allowing them to tell me things that they thought they were protecting me from.

Ironically, as a result of revealing my traumatic ordeal to others, I found my voice. I could now explain the hidden frustrations that had held me in bondage until I was 80 years old.

I was finally able to say, "I know your father was cruel to you. And, *he raped me*! I never deserved to live with a person like that." No one does.

I was also able to discover that in my hurt, I developed a big heart, so that I could reach out to those who found it difficult to move towards a more positive outlook on life.

Rape is a sexual assault forced upon an individual who has not given consent. Thousands of women and men have suffered from this traumatic event. And of these victims, many have managed somehow to live their lives—as normal as their minds would allow. Many remain nameless, never telling a soul. Some have fought back through our justice system. Others have coped through their own self-reliance, where they've addressed the issue head-on, choosing to tell the truth out in the open, in hopes of preventing another attack, and of making the perpetrators pay for the wrong that they inflicted.

In some cases, as in my case, Stockholm Syndrome (S.S.) is the second culprit to deal with in the victim's life. S.S. victims endure additional suffering, as they manage to physically live with and sometimes even marry their assailants.

I wanted to share my story in hopes of helping someone else who may have taken this route. Over 30,000 women have fallen into the S.S. trap.

For me, I was young, with no real life issues to address. As much as the discussion is needed today, in those days, there was thought to be no reason for my parents to sit me down to discuss the issues of rape. I was a good girl who came from a strong family. My dad demonstrated the role of a strong, rational, and protective man in our house. However, the day that I thought I was protecting my family from danger and scandal—by choosing to marry Wadean instead of telling my parents the truth—was the day I lost the good life my parents had planned for me. And for the following 30 years and more, I paid dearly for it. And so did our children and grandchildren.

In the article entitled *The Psychology of Rape*, the author Dr. Wanda Franz, Ph.D., of West Virginia University, explains that rape should be clearly defined as a pseudo-sexual act that has nothing to do with sex; the rape occurs to gratify other needs the rapist has. She further explains that a "power rape" occurs when a rapist plans to attack the victim, and fantasizes about the way his victim will actually *appreciate* and *enjoy* the power he uses to wield control over her.[2] In my case, Wadean did exactly that. He looked for his victim, and found me, even putting on a condom while violating me.

I can't go back and change what happened. It doesn't matter that he never admitted or apologized for all the horrible things he did to me and to our kids. What does matter today is the fact that I was able to come forward and tell the truth, and to chronicle my life in this book. I want to help others avoid years spent wasted in a bad situation.

If you have been a victim of abuse, it is my prayer that this book gives you the courage to speak up. Tell someone what happened to you, so that you can rebuild your life without any more guilt or shame.

Without God, I would not have made it. But because of my desire to know Him more, through His word, I was able to overcome all of my heartache and pain, despite the fact that I once thought I'd never be able to totally recover. May you also know: no matter what adversity you have in your life, you can overcome anything, as I have. With God, anything is possible.

---

[2] Franz, Wanda. "The Psychology of Rape." *Association for Interdisciplinary Research in Values and Social Change*, Summer 2013, v. 25, no. 2, n. pag. *Lifeissues.net*. Web. 22 Aug. 2014.

ABOUT THE AUTHOR

Mary Eatmon was born in March 1931 in Boligee City in Green County, Alabama. As a child, Mary (the eldest of four) had hopes of becoming a woman of influence. As a youth, she accepted her role as a leader and proudly helped wherever she saw her talents were needed. At age 15, Mary ended up having to place any goals she had set on the back burner for at least 50 years because of the tragedy of being raped and eventually marrying her assailant. For 30 years, Mary endured the dysfunctional marriage, as she held on to her integrity. She raised eight children successfully, and she now has over 46 grandchildren.

At age 67, four years after she retired from the Detroit Department of Transportation, Mary completed her Bachelor's Degree in Christian Counseling/Biblical Studies. She is now a licensed minister who maintains five ministries weekly. Over the years, Mary has traveled the world. She's visited exotic lands such as Egypt, Greece, France, Germany, England, and several unique islands. Yet she has found that there is simply no place quite like home. Her stories of adventure, right in her home state of Michigan, visiting its hidden gems, would inspire those who ordinarily would never leave their homes to want to journey to nearby quaint towns to indulge in the beauty of Mackinaw Island, Holland's tulip festival, strawberry-picking in Bellville, and Frankenmuth. When she found out about Michigan's Idlewild and its historical heyday, many of her adult children gleefully vacationed there with her.

Mary's children have watched her approach to life, and have been inspired to love the things that are before them, no matter what those things are. She is well loved and visited often. Mary would often take her young children to Detroit's holiday festivities, a tradition that she carries on with her grandchildren today. Together, they attend the Noel Night as a family. When she's not spending time with family or ministering to the public, Mary enjoys square dancing, as she has for over 26 years.

Mary stands amazed at the hand of God at work in her life: "It's got nothing to do with me. It's all Him. To God be the Glory!"

Appendix

RESOURCES FOR RAPE VICTIMS

The Rape, Abuse & Incest National Network (RAINN)

http://www.rainn.org

A non-profit organization based in Washington, D.C., RAINN operates a national hotline for survivors of sexual assault. The hotline 1-800-656-HOPE offers free, confidential counseling and support 24 hours a day, from anywhere in the country.

RESOURCES FOR DOMESTIC VIOLENCE

National Coalition Against Domestic Violence

http://www.ncadv.org

P.O. Box 18749

Denver, CO 80218

Phone: 1-303-839-1852

RESOURCES FOR CHILD MOLESTATION

Childhelp USA

Hotline: 1-800-4-A-CHILD (422-4453)

The Childhelp USA hotline is a national 24-hour toll-free hotline for child abuse. Its purpose is to take calls from any individuals dealing with abuse, and connect them with the agencies set up to report and deal with abuse in their state and locality.

RESOURCES FOR BIPOLAR DISORDER

SAMHSA (Substance Abuse and Mental Health Services Administration—U.S. Department of Health and Human Services)

http://www.samhsa.gov

Phone: 1-877-726-4727

National Alliance on Mental Illness (NAMI)

http://www.nami.org

Phone: 1-800-950-6264

Millions of Americans are affected by mental illness. NAMI advocates for universal access to treatment, services, support, and research. Contact NAMI to find a chapter in your area.

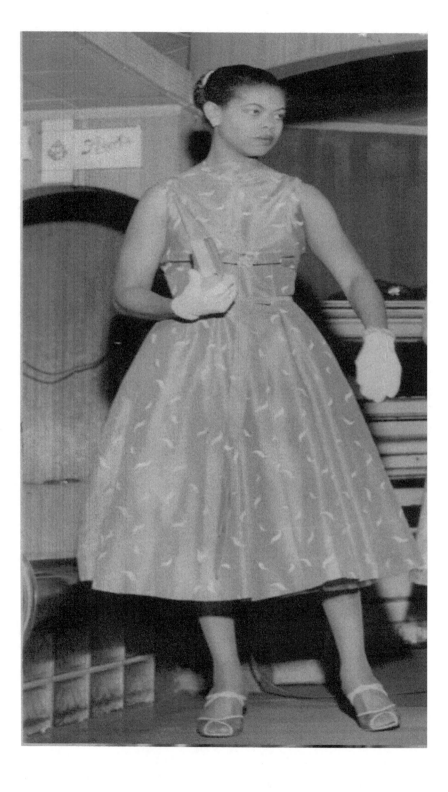

Leave the driving to them

Women man buses

Div. 26 welcomes new members

Some comely young ladies have recently joined the ranks of ATU Div. 26. In the photo at top left is Doris Walker, while Cynthia Jackson (left) and Deborah La Mar are shown in the top right photo. In the bottom picture are: first row, from the left, Bernadine Buffington and Joe Ann Carr; second row, Maxine Bryant, Rose Bernard, Mary Eatmon, and Jerry Jones; in the back row, and enjoying every minute of it, is Div. 26 Correspondent James E. Sims, whose last column appears in this issue. He is giving it up to run for elective office in Div. 26.

Made in the USA
San Bernardino, CA
02 March 2016